Education Station Reading

in collaboration
with Harcourt Achieve

Student Resource Book

ACKNOWLEDGMENTS

Executive Editor: Lynn Fontana, PhD., V.P. of Education, Catapult Learning

Editor: Patricia Hoge, Executive Director of Curriculum and Instruction

Contributing Authors:

Liz Donnegan
Joanie Hedstrom
Ashlie Kauffman
Hannah Magram
Robin Melanson

Lauren Moore
Elisa Oaksmith
Christina Roll
Susan Schuster
Ellen Sugar

Content Editors:

Kathy Blessman
Alice Garten

Patricia Reuss
Karen Zill

Copy Editors:

Sarah Hedges
Doug Mowbray

Amy Peterson

Editorial Advisory Committee:

Richard Bavaria, PhD.
Tracy Broccolino
Virginia Carr
Lynn Fontana
Patricia Hoge

Laurie Layton
Karen Roper
Michele Soussou
Deborah Weil

ISBN 0-7398-9883-3

Printed in the United States of America
6 7 8 9 054 08 07

Contents

Section C

Section D

Contents

Section E

Token Tracker

Name

DATE	TRANSACTION	DEPOSIT +	WITHDRAWAL −	BALANCE =	TEACHER INITIALS

DATE	TRANSACTION	DEPOSIT +	WITHDRAWAL −	BALANCE =	TEACHER INITIALS

Good Reader Strategies
DURING READING

A good reader will:

 look at the picture

 cover up part of the word

 see if the word fits

 sound out the word

 start over when you get stuck

 skip the word and read on

 make a good guess

 read it again

 find little word in a big word

 slow down when it gets hard

How Do I Earn Tokens?

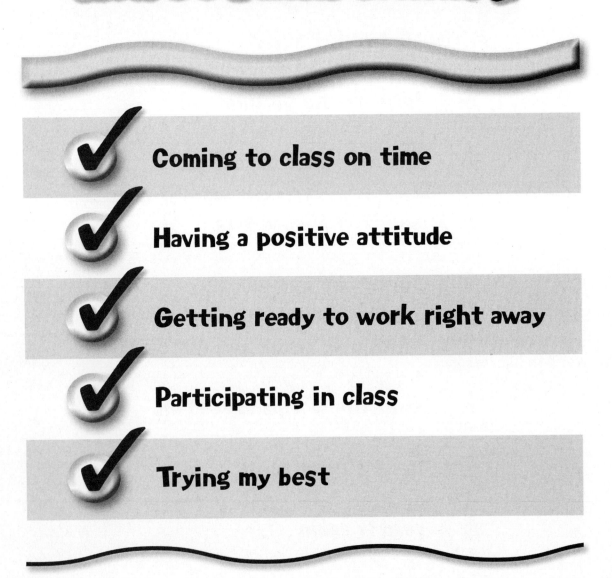

✓ Coming to class on time

✓ Having a positive attitude

✓ Getting ready to work right away

✓ Participating in class

✓ Trying my best

Phonics
(c+at=)

Directions: Read each sentence. Circle the word that completes the sentences. Write the word on the line.

1. Please _____ the water to make tea.   boil/boy

2. Wrap the meat in _____ and broil it.   fall/foil

3. June is a girl, and Bruce is a _____.   boy/bar

4. A car needs gas and _____.   oar/oil

5. I hear too much _____ to take a nap.   noise/nose

6. My baby has a new _____ duck.   toy/tea

7. I need to buy _____ for my plants.   soil/say

8. The pin has a sharp _____.   paint/point

9. I have a new _____.   coal/coin

10. My name is _____.   Roy/Sue

Bonus

Write three sentences using any of the words from your resource sheet.

_____

_____

_____

Fluency Focus

Flea Trip

There once was a dog named Daisy. She had lots of fleas. Old Seth was the oldest flea. Tim, Tom, and Tammy were young fleas.

Daisy's owner looked at her. "I'll take you to the vet," he said. "She'll treat your fleas." And so they went to the vet.

"Help!" cried Old Seth. "The vet will get rid of us!"

"Quick! Jump off!" shouted Tammy.

All the fleas jumped high into the air.

"Whee!" shouted the fleas. "We're flying!"

Then the fleas were falling!

"Help!" shouted the fleas. "We're falling!"

The fleas landed on something furry. "Where are we?" asked Tim.

Old Seth looked around. "We're on a new dog," he said. He gave the dog a little bite. "Not bad!" he said.

"Yippee!" shouted Tim. "We have a new home!"

"Yippee!" shouted the other fleas.

Comprehension

Directions: Use the table below to help you identify the main idea and supporting details of the story.

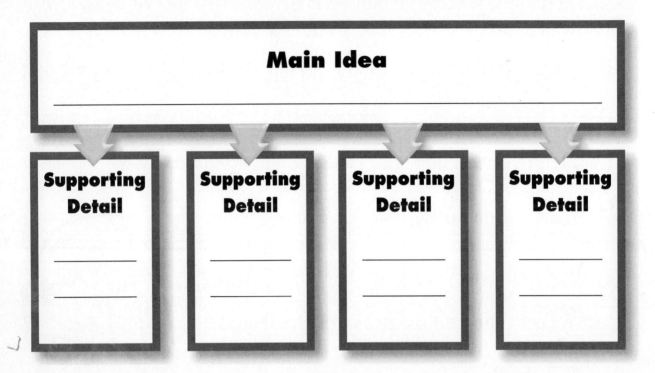

Story

(1) Today was not a good day for Sue. (2) First, she was late for school. (3) Then Sue forgot her homework. (4) She also broke her glasses on the playground. (5) On her way home she fell and cut her knee.

1. Which sentence tells what the whole story is about? Write the number of the sentence that is the main idea on the table top.

2. Which sentences provide details about the story? On each leg of the table, write the number of a sentence that supports the main idea.

Bonus

Write a main idea sentence. You can think about yourself or some one you know.

Vocabulary

Directions: Write a word from the box below that matches each clue.

1. Long, thin parts of an animal's body used for moving or feeling.

   _____

2. The way animals or things get along together.

   _____

3. A strip of rock, sand, or coral close to the surface of a body of water.

   _____

4. A group of plants and animals that need each other.

   _____

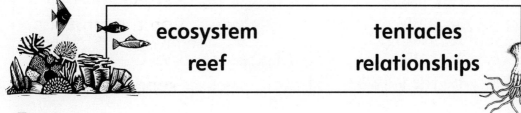

| ecosystem | tentacles |
| reef | relationships |

Bonus

Put the four vocabulary words in alphabetical order in the space below.

Phonics
(c+at= 🐱)

Directions: Think about the vowel sound in *boil* and *boy* as you look at each picture below. Read the words next to each picture and circle the word that matches the picture.

	 coy or coin?		 bay or boy?
	 tie or toil?		 took or toy?
	 broom or broil?		 point or paint?
	 noisy or nosey?		 joy or jam
	 coil or coal?		 poison or person

Try This:
Put "all" in the spaces.

b_____   c_____   w_____

t_____   f_____   sm_____

Fluency Focus

Flea Trip

There once was a dog named Daisy. She had lots of fleas. Old Seth was the oldest flea. Tim, Tom, and Tammy were young fleas.

Daisy's owner looked at her. "I'll take you to the vet," he said. "She'll treat your fleas." And so they went to the vet.

"Help!" cried Old Seth. "The vet will get rid of us!"

"Quick! Jump off!" shouted Tammy.

All the fleas jumped high into the air.

"Whee!" shouted the fleas. "We're flying!"

Then the fleas were falling!

"Help!" shouted the fleas. "We're falling!"

The fleas landed on something furry. "Where are we?" asked Tim.

Old Seth looked around. "We're on a new dog," he said. He gave the dog a little bite. "Not bad!" he said.

"Yippee!" shouted Tim. "We have a new home!"

"Yippee!" shouted the other fleas.

Date:

Focus Skill

Main Idea and Supporting Details
The **main idea** is what an article is about. The **supporting details** tell more about the main idea.

Use the article and the main idea chart to write your answers.

Main Idea

_____

Supporting Detail

_____

_____

Supporting Detail

_____

_____

Supporting Detail

_____

_____

Answer the question below in complete sentences.

1. What might be another good title for this section?

_____

Vocabulary

Directions: Below is a list of the vocabulary words from the article "At Home in a Coral Reef." On the lines below the list, arrange the words in the order in which they appear in the glossary.

- colonies
- reef
- ecosystem
- inactive
- algae
- tentacles
- relationship
- endanger

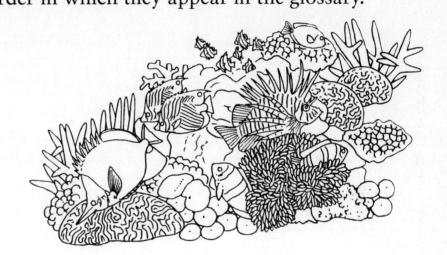

1. _____

2. _____

3. _____

4. _____

5. _____

6. _____

7. _____

8. _____

Phonics
(c+at= 🐱)

Directions: Find as many oi/oy words as you can by drawing lines from one letter to another. You can only use each letter once.

c	o	t	n	l
b	r	a	l	y
u	t	i	y	t
i	n	y	y	
t	a	o	i	
b	o	y	o	
a	n	e	y	
r	e	n	e	
j	o	b	s	
j	i	n	l	
c	o	i	n	

Date:

Fluency Focus

Flea Trip

There once was a dog named Daisy. She had lots of fleas. Old Seth was the oldest flea. Tim, Tom, and Tammy were young fleas.

Daisy's owner looked at her. "I'll take you to the vet," he said. "She'll treat your fleas." And so they went to the vet.

"Help!" cried Old Seth. "The vet will get rid of us!"

"Quick! Jump off!" shouted Tammy.

All the fleas jumped high into the air.

"Whee!" shouted the fleas. "We're flying!"

Then the fleas were falling!

"Help!" shouted the fleas. "We're falling!"

The fleas landed on something furry. "Where are we?" asked Tim.

Old Seth looked around. "We're on a new dog," he said. He gave the dog a little bite. "Not bad!" he said.

"Yippee!" shouted Tim. "We have a new home!"

"Yippee!" shouted the other fleas.

Your Turn to Write

Choose an animal that you think is interesting. Think about where it lives, what it looks like, and how it acts. Then complete the main idea chart below.

Main Idea

A _____ is an interesting animal.

Supporting Detail

_____

_____

Supporting Detail

_____

_____

Supporting Detail

_____

_____

Date: _____

Vocabulary

Directions: Write a word from the box that matches each clue.
Then read the word formed by the boxed letters.

| algae | colonies | ecosystem | reef | relationship | tentacles |

1. Long, thin parts of an animal's body used for moving

   or feeling: ___ ___ ___ ___ ___ [ ] ___ ___ ___

   ₁

2. The way animals or things get along together:

   ___ ___ ___ ___ ___ ___ ___ [ ] ___ ___ ___ ___ ___ ___

   ₂

3. A strip of rock, sand, or coral close to the surface

   of a body of water: [ ] ___ ___ ___

   ₃

4. Water plants: ___ ___ ___ [ ] ___

   ₄

5. Groups that live together: ___ ___ [ ] ___ ___ ___ ___ ___

   ₅

6. A group of plants and animals that need each

   other to live: ___ ___ ___ [ ] ___ ___ ___ ___

   ₆

   ___ ___ ___ ___ ___ ___

   1   2   3   4   5   6

Date: _____

Phonics
(c+at= 🐱)

Directions: 1. Read each sentence.
2. Circle the ou/ow word in the sentence.
3. Print it on the line.

1. I live on the edge of a small town. _____

2. My house is near a park. _____

3. I go outside a lot during the summer. _____

4. From my window, I can see flowers. _____

5. In the summer, I watch the farmer plow his field. _____

6. His car makes a loud noise. _____

7. I can hear owls hooting in the tree. _____

8. I saw a flock of birds flying south. _____

9. Summer is about to start. _____

10. I like to watch clouds. _____

Bonus:

Write some funny sentences. Use "house" and "owl" in one sentence. Use "outside" and "clouds" in your second sentence.

Date:

Fluency Focus

All About Pillbugs

Pillbug Homes

As people, we like our homes to be warm, clean, and dry. A pillbug likes a dark, damp home. If it gets too dry, it dies. The pillbug stays out of the warm sun in the day. It crawls back out when it is dark.

Baby Pillbugs

Baby pillbugs hatch from eggs. They live in dead leaves or under tree bark. Baby pillbugs live with their mother. Most tiny creatures don't see their mother. The mother just lays eggs and moves on. Pillbug mothers stay around!

Did You Know?

The pillbug belongs to the crab and lobster family! Most members of this family live in water and breathe with gills. The pillbug breathes with gills, too.

Comprehension

Characters _____

```
┌─────────────────────────────────────────────────┐
│                    Problem                        │
│  _____ │
│  _____ │
└─────────────────────────────────────────────────┘
```

```
┌─────────────────────────────────────────────────┐
│                    Event 1                        │
│  _____ │
│  _____ │
└─────────────────────────────────────────────────┘
```

```
┌─────────────────────────────────────────────────┐
│                    Event 2                        │
│  _____ │
│  _____ │
└─────────────────────────────────────────────────┘
```

```
┌─────────────────────────────────────────────────┐
│                   Solution                        │
│  _____ │
│  _____ │
└─────────────────────────────────────────────────┘
```

reputation • misunderstanding • cruel • ruined • fragile • rumor • manners

C4

Directions: Select two questions to answer. Circle your choices. Explain your answers below.

Q: Can you think of a misunderstanding that you had with a friend?

Q: Can you think of an animal that is cruel?

Q: Have you ever ruined a dress or a pair of pants?

Q: Have you ever broken anything that was fragile?

Q: Do you have good manners? Do you say "please" and "thank you"?

Q: Do you listen to rumors about your friends or family?

Q: Do people like you? Do you have a good reputation?

A: _____

_____

A: _____

_____

Date:

Phonics

(c+at= )

Directions: Underline the two words in each sentence that have the same vowel sound as "cow" and "out."

1. My pet mouse is brown.

2. The rain came down from the cloud.

3. I plow the ground, so I can grow plants.

4. We are proud of you; take a bow.

5. Do you know how to get to my house?

Date:

Fluency Focus

All About Pillbugs

Pillbug Homes

As people, we like our homes to be warm, clean, and dry. A pillbug likes a dark, damp home. If it gets too dry, it dies. The pillbug stays out of the warm sun in the day. It crawls back out when it is dark.

Baby Pillbugs

Baby pillbugs hatch from eggs. They live in dead leaves or under tree bark. Baby pillbugs live with their mother. Most tiny creatures don't see their mother. The mother just lays eggs and moves on. Pillbug mothers stay around!

Did You Know?

The pillbug belongs to the crab and lobster family! Most members of this family live in water and breathe with gills. The pillbug breathes with gills, too.

Date:

Plot

A **plot** is the important events in a story. All plots have a **beginning,** a **middle,** and an **end.**

Use events from the story to complete the plot chart.

Beginning

_____

Middle

_____

End

_____

_____

Date:

Vocabulary

Read the paragraph. Fill in the circle next to the word that completes each sentence.

Everybody liked Red Riding Hood. She had a _____ 1 for being kind and caring. She was always nice and polite and had good _____ 2 . When she found out that Goldilocks broke into the Bears' house, she wanted to _____ 3 the problem. As it turned out, it was all a big _____ 4 . Baby Bear had actually invited Goldilocks over, but then he forgot!

1.
- ○ story
- ○ reputation
- ○ party
- ○ feeling

2.
- ○ manners
- ○ bicycle
- ○ smile
- ○ books

3.
- ○ excite
- ○ argue
- ○ leave
- ○ resolve

4.
- ○ surprise
- ○ friendship
- ○ happiness
- ○ misunderstanding

Date:

Phonics

$$(c+at=)$$

Directions: Answer *Yes* or *No* to the following questions:

1. Will a cow get a crown for eating a flower?

2. Does a clown jump up and down in the spotlight?

3. Is a brown mouse as big as your bed?

4. Does the toy mouse clean your house with a towel and a broom?

5. Do owls make spooky noises outside at night?

6. Is it cloudy and damp during a rain shower?

7. Do flowers frown?

8. Is a ball round?

9. Do you use a towel to dry off?

10. Do dogs growl?

Date:

Fluency Focus

All About Pillbugs

Pillbug Homes

As people, we like our homes to be warm, clean, and dry. A pillbug likes a dark, damp home. If it gets too dry, it dies. The pillbug stays out of the warm sun in the day. It crawls back out when it is dark.

Baby Pillbugs

Baby pillbugs hatch from eggs. They live in dead leaves or under tree bark. Baby pillbugs live with their mother. Most tiny creatures don't see their mother. The mother just lays eggs and moves on. Pillbug mothers stay around!

Did You Know?

The pillbug belongs to the crab and lobster family! Most members of this family live in water and breathe with gills. The pillbug breathes with gills, too.

Date:

Your Turn to Write

Think about another fairy tale. What would the story be like if the bad character gave his or her point of view? Use the plot chart to plan some different story events.

Beginning

_____

Middle

_____

_____

End

_____

_____

Date:

Vocabulary

C6

Directions: 1. Match the word with its definition.
2. Draw a line from the word to the correct definition.

1. fragile   the way people see and think about someone

2. misunderstood   polite ways to act

3. resolve   a story that has not been proven true

4. manners   mean

5. rumors   harmed or damaged

6. ruined   easy to break

7. cruel   not understood

8. reputation   to settle or solve

Date:

Phonics
$$(c+at=)$$

Directions: Read the sentences below. Notice how the words in the sentence use the al/au/aw digraphs. Underline each word that contains a digraph. Circle 'Yes' or 'No' to answer the questions.

1. Can a hawk do its laundry in a tub?   Yes   No

2. Can Paul enjoy swimming on the lawn?   Yes   No

3. Can a baby crawl faster than a dog can run?   Yes   No

4. Is it helpful to use a lawnmower to cut the grass?   Yes   No

5. Is it your fault if you yawn when you are tired?   Yes   No

Fluency Focus

Weird Weather

Weather happens all over the world. Most of the time, the weather doesn't seem very important to us. But sometimes, the weather gets weird.

The Day It Rained Small Frogs

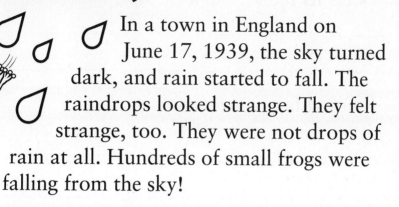

In a town in England on June 17, 1939, the sky turned dark, and rain started to fall. The raindrops looked strange. They felt strange, too. They were not drops of rain at all. Hundreds of small frogs were falling from the sky!

What Happened?

Storms can bring strong winds. Some winds spin around. They start to suck things up from the ground and blow them around in the sky. The things later fall back to the ground, far from where the winds picked them up. This is what happened to the frogs. A storm picked them up from a river, then they fell back to earth.

Date:

Comprehension

Sequence

Writers can tell how to make or do something. They write the **steps** in the **sequence,** or order, in which they happen.

Use the information about making a peanut butter and jelly sandwich to complete the chart.

Step 1 _____

_____

Step 2 _____

_____

Step 3 _____

_____

Step 4 _____

_____

Step 5 _____

_____

Vocabulary

Directions: Review the vocabulary words and their definitions.

Word	Definition
fiesta	a party
traditional	something passed down from parents
mixture	something made by stirring things together
overlap	to lay two things together, partly covering each other
design	to plan how something will look
features	parts of an animal's or person's body
fringe	a row of pieces of fabric or paper that hang down
streamers	long, thin paper strips

C7

Bonus Activity

Directions: Complete each sentence using the words from the list above.

1. My skirt has red _____ at the bottom.

2. The baby has pretty _____.

3. I love to drink milk with chocolate syrup. It is a good _____.

4. When I visit Mexico, I hope that I am invited to a _____.

5. My mother made a new _____ for my dress.

Date:

Phonics
$$(c + at = \text{🐱})$$

Directions: Use the letters s, p, l, r, j, and cl to make 'aw' words.

1. __aw   5. __ __aw

2. __aw   6. __awn

3. __aw   7. __aws

4. __aw   8. __aw

Directions: Use the letters p and c to make 'au' words.

1. __ause   2. __ause

Fluency Focus

Weird Weather

Weather happens all over the world. Most of the time, the weather doesn't seem very important to us. But sometimes, the weather gets weird.

The Day It Rained Small Frogs

In a town in England on June 17, 1939, the sky turned dark, and rain started to fall. The raindrops looked strange. They felt strange, too. They were not drops of rain at all. Hundreds of small frogs were falling from the sky!

C8

What Happened?

Storms can bring strong winds. Some winds spin around. They start to suck things up from the ground and blow them around in the sky. The things later fall back to the ground, far from where the winds picked them up. This is what happened to the frogs. A storm picked them up from a river, then they fell back to earth.

Sequence

Writers can tell how to make or do something. They write the **steps** in the **sequence,** or order, in which they happen.

Use information from the article to complete the chart.
Write the order of the steps to tell how to make a piñata.

Step 1 _____

Step 2 _____

Step 3 _____

Step 4 _____

Step 5 _____

Use the article and your chart to write the answers.

1. What happens before the piñata is filled with treats?

_____

2. In which step do you need to use cardboard?

_____

Date:

Vocabulary

Write the word from the box that completes each sentence.

design   fiesta   mixture   streamers   traditional

1. Mr. Ruiz is planning a _____ to celebrate his son's birthday.

2. He will serve some _____ foods that his father used to make.

3. Mr. Ruiz decides to _____ a piñata to look like a donkey.

4. He adds long paper _____ to hang from the feet of the donkey.

5. Mr. Ruiz fills the piñata with a _____ of toys and treats.

Extend Your Vocabulary

Dictionary Skills: Words in a dictionary appear in alphabetical order. Write each set of words below in alphabetical order.

6. | traditional   streamers   overlap |
   |---|

   a. _____   b. _____   c. _____

7. | fiesta   fringe   features |
   |---|

   a. _____   b. _____   c. _____

C8

Phonics
$$(c+at=\text{🐱})$$

Directions: Fill in the blanks with words from our story. Use the words in the box below.

Paul	paws	all	saucer	squawk
haul	falling	yawn	awful	dawn

1. _____ is my friend.

2. When I am tired, I _____.

3. I broke my mother's cup and _____.

4. My cat's _____ are dirty.

5. Will you _____ the trash away?

6. I don't feel well; I feel _____.

7. _____ of us are going to the beach.

8. When I look up at the stars, I sometimes think that they are _____.

9. Do hawks_____?

10. The boys and girls wanted to camp out until _____.

Date:

Fluency Focus

Weird Weather

Weather happens all over the world. Most of the time, the weather doesn't seem very important to us. But sometimes, the weather gets weird.

The Day It Rained Small Frogs

In a town in England on June 17, 1939, the sky turned dark, and rain started to fall. The raindrops looked strange. They felt strange, too. They were not drops of rain at all. Hundreds of small frogs were falling from the sky!

What Happened?

Storms can bring strong winds. Some winds spin around. They start to suck things up from the ground and blow them around in the sky. The things later fall back to the ground, far from where the winds picked them up. This is what happened to the frogs. A storm picked them up from a river, then they fell back to earth.

Your Turn to Write

Think about something that you like to make. Use the chart below to show the sequence of the steps you take to make it.

Step 1 ______________________________

Step 2 ______________________________

Step 3 ______________________________

Step 4 ______________________________

Step 5 ______________________________

Date:

Vocabulary

Directions: Circle the letter next to the correct meaning of the word.

1. fiesta
   a. a Mexican toy
   b. a party

2. traditional
   a. something passed down from parents
   b. something brand new

3. mixture
   a. a kind of light
   b. something made by stirring things together

4. overlap
   a. to lay two things together, partly covering each other
   b. to take a trip on land

5. design
   a. to sign a contract
   b. to plan how something will look

6. features
   a. make-believe creatures
   b. parts of an animal's or person's body

7. fringe
   a. a row of pieces of fabric or paper that hang down
   b. a cold place to store food

8. streamers
   a. special pots for cooking vegetables
   b. long, thin paper strips

Phonics

$$(c + at = \text{🐱})$$

Directions: Say the name of each picture. Print its beginning
blend on the line.

Bonus: Write the word on the line that answers the riddle. The
picture will help you.

Sometimes I ring.
Sometimes I chime.
I tick-tock all the time.

_____

Date:

Fluency Focus

Hairem Scarem

There once lived a hairem scarem. He had really long hair all over his head and body. He never cut the hair. He just let it grow.

His hair was a real mess, but the animals did not dare tell him so. Lizards got lost in it. Monkeys got mixed up in it.

A turtle once tripped on the hairem scarem's hair. The angry turtle cried, "Get your hair cut!"

Then the hairem scarem went for a walk. His hair snagged a snake.

"Get your hair cut!" yelled the snake.

That night, the hairem scarem went to the turtle and the snake. They woke up with long hair stuck to their head.

The Hair Queen was in charge of how the animals looked. She was angry when she saw what the hairem scarem had done. She made him cut off all his hair.

He then looked much smaller. The animals were not afraid of him.

"You're not a hairem scarem!" cried the elephant. "You're a hairless scareless!"

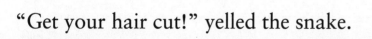

Date:

Comprehension

Make Predictions

Writers give clues in the story about what will happen next. These clues help readers make a **prediction.**

Complete the chart. Use details from "Dante's Lunch" that gave clues about what happened in the story.

What I Predicted

_____

Clues That Helped Me Predict

1. _____

2. _____

3. _____

What I Know Happened

_____

_____

Date:

Vocabulary

Directions: Read each vocabulary word and its definition in the Vocabulary Box below.

Vocabulary Box	
celebration	a special event or day
council	a group that makes decisions
exhausted	very tired
jealous	wanting what someone else has
messenger	someone sent to give information
overjoyed	very happy
scampered	ran quickly
scheme	a plan

C10

Phonics
$(c+at=)$

Directions: Circle all of the words that have the 'tw' blend and the initial /l/ blend.

1. The twins flew over the clouds in the sky.

2. The flounder floundered in the water.

3. The mouse sat on a twitching elephant.

4. The flower said hello to the plant.

5. The twigs jumped over the flock of birds.

6. The plow rolled down the highway,
   while the clown danced.

7. The star twinkled to the boy and girl below.

BONUS: Find the word in the box below that answers each
riddle. Write it on the line.

1. I am in the sky.
   Sometimes I bring you rain.
   What am I?

2. There are two of us.
   We are in the same family
   We look the same.
   Who are we?

_____   _____

cloud	twins	flower

Fluency Focus

Hairem Scarem

There once lived a hairem scarem. He had really long hair all over his head and body. He never cut the hair. He just let it grow.

His hair was a real mess, but the animals did not dare tell him so. Lizards got lost in it. Monkeys got mixed up in it.

A turtle once tripped on the hairem scarem's hair. The angry turtle cried, "Get your hair cut!"

Then the hairem scarem went for a walk. His hair snagged a snake.

"Get your hair cut!" yelled the snake.

That night, the hairem scarem went to the turtle and the snake. They woke up with long hair stuck to their head.

The Hair Queen was in charge of how the animals looked. She was angry when she saw what the hairem scarem had done. She made him cut off all his hair.

He then looked much smaller. The animals were not afraid of him.

"You're not a hairem scarem!" cried the elephant. "You're a hairless scareless!"

Make Predictions

Writers give clues in the story about what will happen next. These clues help readers make a **prediction.**

Use clues from the story to complete the chart.

What I Predicted

_____

Clues That Helped Me Predict

1. _____
2. _____
3. _____

What I Know Happened

_____

_____

Use the story and your chart to write the answers.

1. Why do you think the author says that Rabbit likes to play tricks?

_____

_____

2. How did Rabbit get Otter to take off her fur coat?

_____

Vocabulary

Directions: Draw a line to match each word to its definition.

celebration	a plan
council	wanting what someone else has
exhausted	very happy
jealous	ran quickly
messenger	a special event
overjoyed	a group that makes decisions
scampered	very tired
scheme	someone sent to give information

C11

Phonics
(c + at = 🐱)

Directions: Look at the words in each box. Select the blend to the complete the word. Write the blend in the blank spaces and read each word.

1. __ed	2. __inkle	3. __ock	4. __in	5. __inky	6. __enty
sl tw pl	sl tw bl	bl tw sl	fl tw sl	fl sl pl	fl tw sl
7. __ist	8. __ight	9. __ash	10. __ue	11. __ower	12. __oud
sl tw pl	cl tw fl	pl tw fl	cl tw pl	cl tw fl	cl tw bl

Practice saying these silly sentences with a partner.

1. The twelve black twirling blocks slipped twice.

2. The twins twirled twelve times to the tune of Blinky's music.

3. Twenty flowers twisted in the wind.

4. The plane flew twenty times in the terrible dark night.

5. The sled fled from the twenty-two twins.

Date:

Fluency Focus

Hairem Scarem

There once lived a hairem scarem. He had really long hair all over his head and body. He never cut the hair. He just let it grow.

His hair was a real mess, but the animals did not dare tell him so. Lizards got lost in it. Monkeys got mixed up in it.

A turtle once tripped on the hairem scarem's hair. The angry turtle cried, "Get your hair cut!"

Then the hairem scarem went for a walk. His hair snagged a snake.

C12

"Get your hair cut!" yelled the snake.

That night, the hairem scarem went to the turtle and the snake. They woke up with long hair stuck to their head.

The Hair Queen was in charge of how the animals looked. She was angry when she saw what the hairem scarem had done. She made him cut off all his hair.

He then looked much smaller. The animals were not afraid of him.

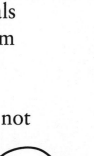

"You're not a hairem scarem!" cried the elephant. "You're a hairless scareless!"

Your Turn to Write

Choose an animal. Use the chart to plan a trick that Rabbit could play on your animal. The trick should explain why your animal looks or acts a certain way.

My Prediction

_____

_____

Clues That Help Predict

1. _____

2. _____

3. _____

4. _____

What Happens

_____

Date:

Vocabulary

Read the paragraph. Fill in the circle next to the word that completes each sentence.

The animal _____ sat around a fire. They were planning a
_____ that would last for three days. Rabbit was sent to invite all
the animals. Bear watched as Rabbit ran away to share the news.
Bear wanted to be a _____, too. He was _____ that Rabbit had
long legs. He wanted to run fast like Rabbit.

1. A   scheme
   B   couch
   C   council
   D   town

2. E   messenger
   F   camp
   G   house
   H   celebration

3. A   messenger
   B   singer
   C   swimmer
   D   dancer

4. E   surprised
   F   overjoyed
   G   jealous
   H   happy

C12

Extend Your Vocabulary

Synonyms Synonyms are words that have almost the same meaning.

Circle the two words in each row that are synonyms.

5. scheme   map   plan   tribe
6. happy   sad   overjoyed   silly
7. hid   scampered   swam   ran
8. lonely   exhausted   excited   tired

Phonics

$$(c + at =)$$

Directions: Match the words that have the same beginning consonant sound. On each line, write the matching word's corresponding letter.

1. this _____   A. sheep

2. wheat _____   B. chin

3. shelf _____   C. then

4. chain _____   D. wheel

Directions: Match the words that have the same ending consonant sound. On each line, write the matching word's corresponding letter.

5. rock _____   A. teach

6. long _____   B. dash

7. beach _____   C. back

8. brush _____   D. sing

Bonus Activity

Unscramble the words in each group to make a sentence.

1. witch   west   went   which

_____?

2. thanked   tourists   Ted   thirty

_____.

Date:

Fluency Focus

Hair Care

We all have hair. We take care of our hair. We care about how it looks. Romans who lived 2,000 years ago took care of their hair, too. They brushed and combed it often. But they washed it only once a year!

Today, we brush and comb our hair often. We also wash our hair often. We use all kinds of things to help make it look nice.

Hair grows every day. The hair on our head grows about 6 inches in a year. Hair grows faster on warm days. It also grows faster when we sleep.

If we do not want long hair, we have to cut it. About 150 years ago, men and boys had their hair cut by barbers. They all had the same haircut. It was short at the back and sides.

Today, many men and women get their hair cut by a hairdresser. Hairdressers wash and cut hair. They color, curl, and style hair, too. But barbers still cut and style hair for men and boys!

C13

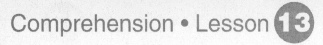

Comprehension

Directions: Fill in the Venn Diagram. On the Basketball side, write details that are true of basketball, but not soccer. On the Soccer side, write details that are true of soccer, but not basketball. In the area where the circles overlap, write the details that are true of both sports.

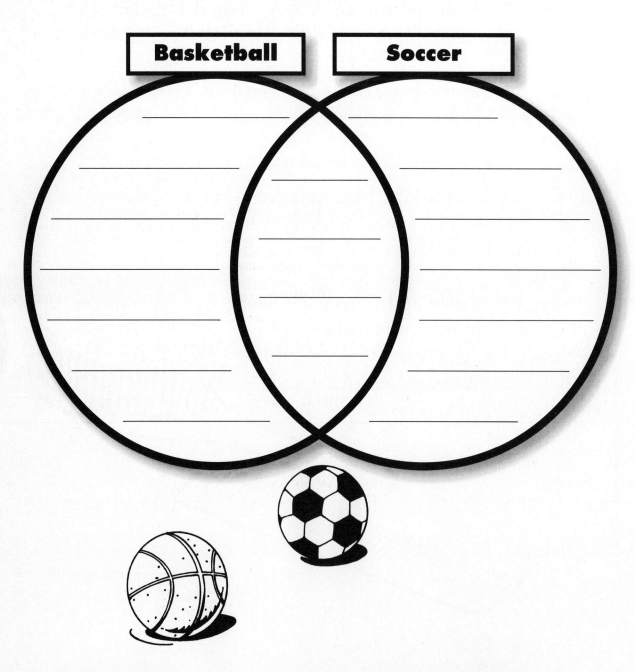

Date:

Vocabulary

Directions: Read each word and its definition presented in the Vocabulary Word Box.

Vocabulary Word Box

camouflage	coloring or body parts that help an animal look like its surroundings
crest	part of an animal's body that rises above its head
prey	an animal that is hunted for food
grasp	to take hold of
scales	thin flat plates that cover the body of some animals
shed	to lose or fall off naturally
predator	an animal that hunts other animals for food
sway	to move back and forth

C13

Phonics
(c+at=🐱)

Directions: Read each word in the box. If the consonant digraph is at the beginning of a word, print the word in the first column. If it is at the end, print the word in the second column.

cheer	dish	quack	peach
teeth	while	wash	chip
shell	thin	duck	touch

Beginning	Ending

Date:

Fluency Focus

Hair Care

We all have hair. We take care of our hair. We care about how it looks. Romans who lived 2,000 years ago took care of their hair, too. They brushed and combed it often. But they washed it only once a year!

Today, we brush and comb our hair often. We also wash our hair often. We use all kinds of things to help make it look nice.

Hair grows every day. The hair on our head grows about 6 inches in a year. Hair grows faster on warm days. It also grows faster when we sleep.

If we do not want long hair, we have to cut it. About 150 years ago, men and boys had their hair cut by barbers. They all had the same haircut. It was short at the back and sides.

Today, many men and women get their hair cut by a hairdresser. Hairdressers wash and cut hair. They color, curl, and style hair, too. But barbers still cut and style hair for men and boys!

C14

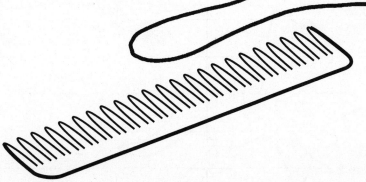

Compare and Contrast

Writers **compare** to show how two or more things are alike. They **contrast** to show how the things are different.

Directions: In the diagram below, provide details about how frilled lizards and veiled chameleons are alike and different.

FRILLED LIZARD — fast runner

BOTH — scales

VEILED CHAMELEON — moves slowly

Date:

Vocabulary

Write the words from the box to complete the story.

camouflage	crest	grasp	predator	prey	sway

A veiled chameleon was warming itself in the sun. Suddenly, it spotted a scary _____ looking for food. The

1

lizard did not want to be the bird's _____. The

2

chameleon slowly wrapped its tail around a tree branch. Then it used its long claws to _____ the branch. The

3

chameleon began to _____ slowly. With its

4

bright colors and the _____ on its head, the

5

chameleon looked just like a leaf. The chameleon had used _____ to save its life.

6

Answer one of the questions below in complete sentences. Use some of the vocabulary from today's lesson.

1. Why would the open flap of skin on the frilled lizard scare away a predator?

_____

_____

2. Why do you think the veiled chameleon wraps its tail around a tree branch when it hunts for food?

_____

_____

Date:

C14

Phonics
$$\left(c + at = \right)$$

Directions: Look at the picture in each box. Complete the word that names the picture by adding the digraph to the word.

ch	th	sh	ck	nk	ng

ba____

so____

mo____

wi____

bru____

____eese

____ain

____eep

tee____

Date:

Fluency Focus

Hair Care

We all have hair. We take care of our hair. We care about how it looks. Romans who lived 2,000 years ago took care of their hair, too. They brushed and combed it often. But they washed it only once a year!

Today, we brush and comb our hair often. We also wash our hair often. We use all kinds of things to help make it look nice.

Hair grows every day. The hair on our head grows about 6 inches in a year. Hair grows faster on warm days. It also grows faster when we sleep.

If we do not want long hair, we have to cut it. About 150 years ago, men and boys had their hair cut by barbers. They all had the same haircut. It was short at the back and sides.

Today, many men and women get their hair cut by a hairdresser. Hairdressers wash and cut hair. They color, curl, and style hair, too. But barbers still cut and style hair for men and boys!

C15

Your Turn to Write

Choose either the frilled lizard or the veiled chameleon. Then choose another animal that you know about. Use the diagram below to compare and contrast the two.

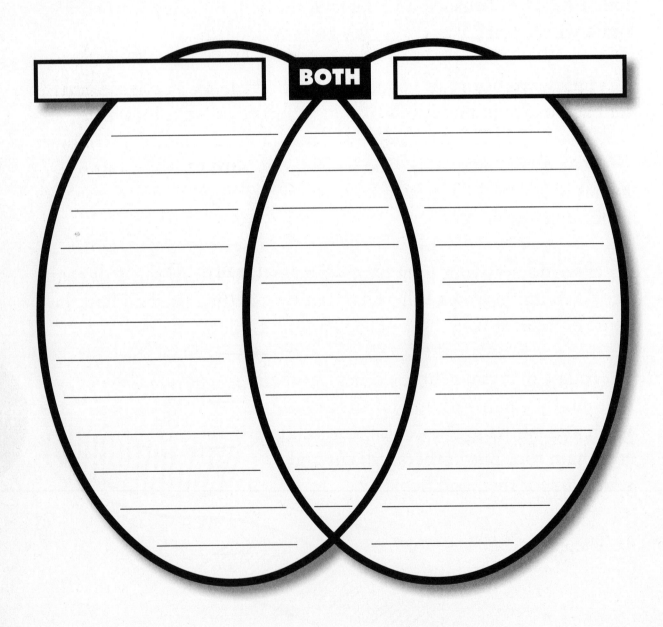

BOTH

Date:

Extend Your Vocabulary

Words That Have Two Meanings

Some words can have more than one meaning.

Read each word and its meanings. Write the letter of the meaning for each underlined word.

> **scales a.** Thin, flat plates that cover the body of some animals. **b.** Tools used to find out how much things weigh.
>
> **shed c.** To lose or fall off naturally. **d.** A small building that is used to store things.

1. We looked for a hammer inside the tool <u>shed</u>. _____

2. The farmer used <u>scales</u> to weigh the fruit. _____

3. The young lizard was about to <u>shed</u> its skin. _____

4. The garden snake had smooth, dry <u>scales</u>. _____

C15

Phonics

$$(c+at=)$$

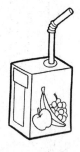

Directions: 1. Underline the ue, ui, or ew digraph in each word as you read it.

2. Draw a line to the picture that matches each word.

suit

fruit

juice

screw

glue

Date:

Fluency Focus

The Missing Mystery

Detective Fogtop picked up the ringing phone. "Detective Fogtop, mystery solver," he said.

A woman's voice said, "This is Rita Romero, the mystery writer. Someone stole my new mystery story! I'm being interviewed right now. Violet Snippy is here from the local newspaper. Can you come over in one hour? "

"I'll be there," Detective Fogtop said.

Detective Fogtop walked up the steps of Miss Romero's front porch. A woman burst out the front door. It was Violet Snippy. She crashed right into Detective Fogtop. They both fell down the steps. Violet Snippy dropped a paper bag.

Fogtop tried to help her pick up the bag. They both reached for it at the same time.

"Give me that!" Violet shouted, grabbing the bag. It ripped open. A compact disk fell out, and papers flew everywhere. Violet grabbed at them.

Hearing the noise, Rita came outside. "It's my mystery!" she said. "Violet Snippy had it all the time! Thank you, Detective Fogtop," she said. "You are the best detective ever."

C16

Comprehension

Directions: Fill in the chart below using information from the story about Jamal.

Clues from Reading

____

____

____

What I Already Know

____

____

____

My Conclusion

____

____

____

Date:

Vocabulary

Directions: Draw a line from the vocabulary word to its definition.

hopeless   playful and full of energy

lead   feeling like the worst will happen

successful   people who find information and solve crimes

nocturnal   helpful information; a clue

detectives   not able to cause damage

fearful   afraid

frisky   doing well

harmless   active at night

C16

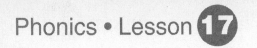

Directions: Underline the words in each sentence that contain the vowel digraphs ue/ui/ew.

1. We will leave for the cruise on Tuesday.

2. Mr. Smith owns three blue suits.

3. The police found a clue to the missing jewels.

4. The crew of the ship had to rescue the swimmers.

5. The artist drew a few pictures of tropical fruits.

6. Sam is a shrewd detective.

7. Annie fell and got a bruise on her leg.

8. It's true—ripe peaches are very juicy.

BONUS
Directions: Whisper Read these words:

crew	cruise	true
few	juicy	clue
shrewd	suits	rescue
drew	bruise	blue
jewels	fruits	Tuesday

Fluency Focus

The Missing Mystery

Detective Fogtop picked up the ringing phone. "Detective Fogtop, mystery solver," he said.

A woman's voice said, "This is Rita Romero, the mystery writer. Someone stole my new mystery story! I'm being interviewed right now. Violet Snippy is here from the local newspaper. Can you come over in one hour? "

"I'll be there," Detective Fogtop said.

Detective Fogtop walked up the steps of Miss Romero's front porch. A woman burst out the front door. It was Violet Snippy. She crashed right into Detective Fogtop. They both fell down the steps. Violet Snippy dropped a paper bag.

Fogtop tried to help her pick up the bag. They both reached for it at the same time.

"Give me that!" Violet shouted, grabbing the bag. It ripped open. A compact disk fell out, and papers flew everywhere. Violet grabbed at them.

Hearing the noise, Rita came outside. "It's my mystery!" she said. "Violet Snippy had it all the time! Thank you, Detective Fogtop," she said. "You are the best detective ever."

C17

Draw Conclusions

Readers **draw conclusions** by thinking about clues or facts in a story and by using what they already know.

Directions: Fill in the chart. Write the clues that helped you draw conclusions.

Clues from Reading	What I Already Knew
Snowball lost her collar.	A cat without a collar might be lost.

My Conclusion

Directions: Use the story and your chart to write the answers.

1. Why didn't Sara recognize Snowball at first?

_____

2. How did Alex explain what happened to Snowball?

_____

_____

Date:

Vocabulary

hopeless	lead	harmless	fearful	nocturnal
frisky	detectives	successful		

Directions: Write the vocabulary word that completes each
sentence.

1. My dog is so _____, I have a difficult time taking her
for a walk.

2. My neighbor says her dog is _____, but to be safe she
keeps her in a fenced-in yard.

3. I have to admit I am a bit _____ of that dog because
it barks all the time.

BONUS:

Directions: Create a sentence using each of the vocabulary
words below.

hopeless _____

_____

successful _____

_____

C17

Date:

Phonics

$$(c + at = \text{🐱})$$

Directions: Complete each sentence with a word from the box.

Part 1

1. Is that a _____ story?

2. I love to look at the _____ sky.

3. _____ I am going to school.

4. Her name is _____ .

Sue
Tuesday
blue
true

Part 2

1. The supermarket sells many _____ and vegetables.

2. The man who owns the supermarket wears a blue _____ .

3. They are hoping to go on a _____ .

4. I forgot to buy _____ when I was there.

fruits
cruise
suit
juice

Part 3

1. Susan owns a _____ shop.

2. The shop is filled with _____ objects every Monday.

3. Each Sunday, Sue puts an ad in the _____ .

4. Sue _____ that her jewelry shop would do very well.

newspaper
new
knew
jewelry

Date:

Fluency Focus

The Missing Mystery

Detective Fogtop picked up the ringing phone. "Detective Fogtop, mystery solver," he said.

A woman's voice said, "This is Rita Romero, the mystery writer. Someone stole my new mystery story! I'm being interviewed right now. Violet Snippy is here from the local newspaper. Can you come over in one hour? "

"I'll be there," Detective Fogtop said.

Detective Fogtop walked up the steps of Miss Romero's front porch. A woman burst out the front door. It was Violet Snippy. She crashed right into Detective Fogtop. They both fell down the steps. Violet Snippy dropped a paper bag.

Fogtop tried to help her pick up the bag. They both reached for it at the same time.

"Give me that!" Violet shouted, grabbing the bag. It ripped open. A compact disk fell out, and papers flew everywhere. Violet grabbed at them.

Hearing the noise, Rita came outside. "It's my mystery!" she said. "Violet Snippy had it all the time! Thank you, Detective Fogtop," she said. "You are the best detective ever."

C18

Think about something you have that is important to you. Suppose it is missing. What could have happened to it? What clues might help you find it?

Clues

_____

_____

_____

_____

_____

What I Already Know

_____

_____

_____

_____

_____

My Conclusion

_____

_____

_____

_____

_____

Date:

Vocabulary

Fill in the circle next to the correct answer.

1. In this story, <u>frisky</u> means—
   - Ⓐ missing
   - Ⓑ playful
   - Ⓒ sad
   - Ⓓ lost

2. In this story, <u>detectives</u> means—
   - Ⓔ people who cook food
   - Ⓕ people who write books
   - Ⓖ people who paint
   - Ⓗ people who find information

3. In this story, <u>nocturnal</u> means—
   - Ⓐ something that eats garbage
   - Ⓑ something that is active at night
   - Ⓒ something that smells really bad
   - Ⓓ something that is missing

4. In this story, <u>lead</u> means—
   - Ⓔ metal
   - Ⓕ follow
   - Ⓖ clue
   - Ⓗ show

Extend Your Vocabulary

Suffixes A suffix is a word part that is added to the end of a word. A suffix changes the meaning of a word.

less = without	ful = full of

Circle the suffix in each word. Write the meaning of each word on the line.

5. fearful _____

6. harmless _____

7. hopeless _____

8. successful _____

C18

Date: _____

Phonics

$$(\text{c+at=} \text{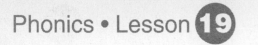})$$

Directions: Read each sentence. Choose the best word to complete
the sentence. Circle the word and write it on the line.

1. Our group _____ for races all last spring.
   (trains, trained, training)

2. When the wind blew, the open door _____ shut.
   (slams, slammed, slamming)

3. Every time Allison _____ in those shoes, she gets a
   blister on her foot. (dances, danced, dancing)

4. Yesterday, my dog _____ into my arms.
   (jumps, jumped, jumping)

5. Manuel is _____ the windows because it is starting
   to rain. (closes, closed, closing)

6. That movie was so funny; we _____ and
   _____. (laughs, laughed, laughing)

7. I _____ all day and I am very tired.
   (works, worked, working)

8. He is _____ in the city. (lives, lived, living)

9. He _____ at the book yesterday.
   (looks, looked, looking)

Date:

Fluency Focus

The First Telephone Call

Alexander Graham Bell and his helper, Thomas Watson, worked together on an important invention. They made a machine that used electricity to carry speech sounds along a wire. The machine was the first telephone.

Another inventor was also working on a machine that used electricity to carry speech sounds. His name was Elisha Gray. Both Bell and Gray tried to be the first to finish their invention, but Bell won the race.

On March 10, 1876, Alexander Graham Bell made the first telephone call ever. He spoke to Thomas Watson. Watson was in another room. Bell said, "Mr. Watson, come here. I want to see you."

Watson rushed into the room. He had heard Bell's voice over the wire! Both men were very excited.

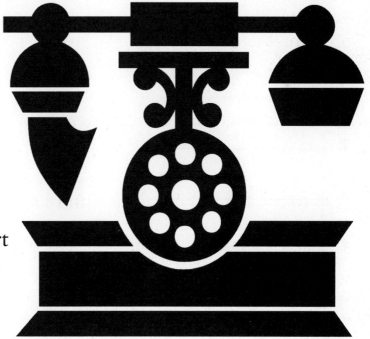

Because of Bell, people near each other or far apart can talk to each other. The telephone brings together people from all over the world.

C19

Comprehension

Directions: For the sentences below, fill in some facts and opinions about you by adding details to each blank.

1. My name is _____.

2. I am _____ years old.

3. I have _____ brothers and _____ sisters.

4. I think the most delicious food is _____.

5. I like to play _____.

6. The best sport is _____.

For each sentence above, write if the sentence is a fact or your opinion.

1. _____

2. _____

3. _____

4. _____

5. _____

6. _____

Vocabulary

Directions: Read the words and definitions aloud with the teacher.

equator	the imaginary line around the center of the Earth
tropics	the very hot area near the equator, or center of the Earth
canopy	a covering or top layer
dense	very thick
species	groups of living things that have some of the same features
extinct	no longer living
destruction	the act of ruining something
native	person born in a certain place

C19

Directions: The words listed below are hidden in the puzzle. Each word has an inflectional ending, -s, -ed, or -ing, added to it. Find and circle the word and word ending in the puzzle and write it on the line provided.

```
c   a   m   p   e   d
h   r   u   n   s   t
a   h   i   k   e   d
n   k   p   d   m   e
g   n   i   a   e   e
i   o   c   t   e   m
n   w   k   e   t   p
g   s   s   i   s   u
```

camp _____

change _____

run _____

hike _____

know _____

pick _____

meet _____

Date:

Fluency Focus

The First Telephone Call

Alexander Graham Bell and his helper, Thomas Watson, worked together on an important invention. They made a machine that used electricity to carry speech sounds along a wire. The machine was the first telephone.

Another inventor was also working on a machine that used electricity to carry speech sounds. His name was Elisha Gray. Both Bell and Gray tried to be the first to finish their invention, but Bell won the race.

On March 10, 1876, Alexander Graham Bell made the first telephone call ever. He spoke to Thomas Watson. Watson was in another room. Bell said, "Mr. Watson, come here. I want to see you."

Watson rushed into the room. He had heard Bell's voice over the wire! Both men were very excited.

Because of Bell, people near each other or far apart can talk to each other. The telephone brings together people from all over the world.

C20

Fact and Opinion

Facts are statements that can be proven. **Opinions** are a person's beliefs or feelings. Opinions cannot be proven.

Use the article to fill in the chart. In the first column, write sentences from the article. Decide if each sentence is a fact or an opinion. Then write a sentence to tell how you know.

Sentence	Fact or Opinion	How I Know
1. You won't find a more interesting place anywhere else on Earth!	opinion	It is a belief that cannot be proven.
2. Most rainforests are found near the Equator.		
3.		
4.		

Write one opinion that the writer has. Then explain why you think this is an opinion.

5. The writer believes that _____.

6. I think it is an opinion because _____.

Date:

Vocabulary

Directions: Complete each sentence with a word from the vocabulary list below.

1. Dinosaurs are _____ animals.

2. South America is south of the _____.

3. The periwinkle is a _____ plant of the rain forest.

4. At the school picnic, there was a _____ over the food to protect it from the sun.

5. The woods near my house are very _____.

6. Once the wrecking crew arrived, the _____ of the building began.

7. Hurricanes begin in the warm ocean waters in the _____.

8. Some unusual animal _____ live in Australia.

VOCABULARY LIST

canopy
dense
destruction
equator
extinct
native
species
tropics

C20

81

Word Study

Word	Word Divided into Syllables
1. better	
2. ribbons	
3. princess	
4. chimney	
5. often	
6. puddle	
7. chamber	
8. gallon	
9. mitten	
10. confuse	

Date:

Fluency Focus

Something to Chew On

Do you like to chew gum? What is your favorite flavor or brand? Did you know that people who lived very long ago also liked to chew gum? For a long time, we thought the habit went back only one hundred years or so. More recent discoveries show that gum chewing is at least 9,000 years old. People who lived thousands of years ago chewed black lumps of tar that came from birch trees. Why did they do it? Scientists don't know for sure. People back then might have chewed the tar to clean their teeth. They might have been trying to help a hurting tooth. Or perhaps they just liked the taste. Would you be surprised to learn that most of the early people who chewed gum were between the ages of 6 and 15? How old do you think most people are who chew gum today? Now that's a thought to chew on!

Date:

Main Idea and Supporting Details

The **main idea** is the most important idea of an article or a paragraph. **Supporting details** tell more about the main idea.

Directions: Use information from the paragraph to complete the main idea chart. Write the main idea and supporting details.

Main Idea

_____

_____

Supporting Detail 1

_____

_____

Supporting Detail 2

_____

_____

Supporting Detail 3

_____

_____

Date:

Vocabulary

Directions: Write words from the box to complete the paragraph.

excess	fads	generations	protests

   I can understand why my parents ask me to clean up my room. It's a mess. There's _____ stuff everywhere. However, what I can't understand are their _____ about what kids my age wear. That's when I take out photos of Mom and Dad when they were my age. I point out how weird the fashion _____ of their time were. I guess all _____ have different ideas about what's cool!

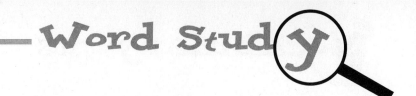

Word Study

Directions: In each sentence below, circle the word with the two consonants together. Then write the word on the line and divide it into syllables.

1. John wants to be the drummer in his high school band.

   _____

2. Dad has to clean the leaves out of the gutters so they don't

   clog. _____

3. The traffic always gets heavy at five o'clock. _____

4. If you hold a shell up to your ear, you can listen to the ocean.

   _____

5. Don broke a car window when he hit a homerun.

   _____

Fluency Focus

Something to Chew On

Do you like to chew gum? What is your favorite flavor or brand? Did you know that people who lived very long ago also liked to chew gum? For a long time, we thought the habit went back only one hundred years or so. More recent discoveries show that gum chewing is at least 9,000 years old. People who lived thousands of years ago chewed black lumps of tar that came from birch trees. Why did they do it? Scientists don't know for sure. People back then might have chewed the tar to clean their teeth. They might have been trying to help a hurting tooth. Or perhaps they just liked the taste. Would you be surprised to learn that most of the early people who chewed gum were between the ages of 6 and 15? How old do you think most people are who chew gum today? Now that's a thought to chew on!

Date:

Main Idea and Supporting Details

The **main idea** is the most important idea of an article or a paragraph. **Supporting details** tell more about the main idea.

Use information from the article to complete the main idea chart. Write the main idea and two more supporting details.

Main Idea

_____

_____

Supporting Detail 1

In the 1950s, rock-and-roll inspired 'bobby-soxer' fashions.

Supporting Detail 2

_____

Supporting Detail 3

_____

Use the article and your main idea chart to write the answers.

1. What might be another good title for this article?

_____

_____

2. How do the details support the main idea?

_____

_____

Dictionary Skills: Guide words tell the first and last entry words on a dictionary page. All of the other words on the page are in alphabetical order between the two guide words.

Circle the letter next to the correct pair of guide words for each word or words.

5. prosper
   a. prospect | proven
   b. propel | prose
   c. provide | public

6. civil rights
   a. children | choice
   b. chunk | circle
   c. citrus | claim

7. authority
   a. atomic | attract
   b. attractive | authorize
   c. autobiography | avoid

8. revolution
   a. revise | rhinoceros
   b. restrain | retreat
   c. rig | rinse

Date: _____

Directions: For each bolded word below, circle the word that is divided correctly.

1. **service**

ser/vice	serv/ice

2. **sudden**

su/dden	sud/den

3. **magnet**

ma/gnet	mag/net

4. **goblin**

gob/lin	gobl/in

5. **servant**

ser/vant	serv/ant

6. **picture**

pict/ure	pic/ture

7. **anger**

an/ger	ang/er

8. **angel**

ang/el	an/gel

9. **doctor**

doc/tor	doct/or

10. **admire**

ad/mire	a/dmire

Date:

Fluency Focus

Something to Chew On

Do you like to chew gum? What is your favorite flavor or brand? Did you know that people who lived very long ago also liked to chew gum? For a long time, we thought the habit went back only one hundred years or so. More recent discoveries show that gum chewing is at least 9,000 years old. People who lived thousands of years ago chewed black lumps of tar that came from birch trees. Why did they do it? Scientists don't know for sure. People back then might have chewed the tar to clean their teeth. They might have been trying to help a hurting tooth. Or perhaps they just liked the taste. Would you be surprised to learn that most of the early people who chewed gum were between the ages of 6 and 15? How old do you think most people are who chew gum today? Now that's a thought to chew on!

Date:

Your Turn to Write

What do you think future generations will say about today's fashion fads? Use the chart to write your main idea and three details that support it.

Main Idea

____

Supporting Detail

____

____

Supporting Detail

____

Supporting Detail

____

____

 Date:

Directions: Select four of the words from the vocabulary words below. Write a sentence using the word in the box provided.

Authority	Civil Rights
Excess	Fads
Generations	Prosper
Protests	Revolution

Word Study

Directions: 1. Divide each word into syllables.

2. Indicate if the first vowel is long or short.

3. Write the number of syllables in each word.

Word	First Vowel Sound	Syllables
si / lent		
ris / en		
pal / ace		
mod / ern		
re / lay		
e / late		
lem / on		
vis / it		
de / cide		
o / ver		

Bonus:

1. limit
2. label
3. music
4. salad
5. metal
6. paper

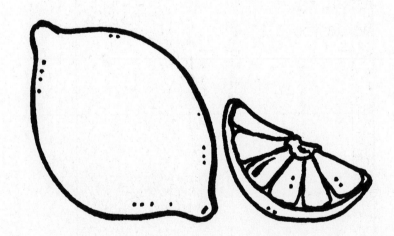

Date:

Fluency Focus

Sparkling Teeth

The Maya were a group of people who lived hundreds of years ago. They lived in the area that is now Central America. The Maya are famous today for their beautiful cities and their written language. They also are known to have taken great pride in their appearance. Mayan men and women often wore jewelry in their lips, noses, and ears.

Teeth were important to the Mayan people. They chewed food with their teeth, of course, but they also decorated them. Some Maya had jewels put into their teeth to improve their looks. First, a hole was drilled into a tooth. Then, a jewel was fit into the hole. The jewel could be a piece of gold, or it could be a shiny red, green, or blue stone. Getting a jewel set into one's tooth was not easy or even very safe. There was a risk of losing the tooth. One slip, and the tooth could be destroyed.

D4

Comprehension

Plot

A **plot** tells what happens at the **beginning, middle,** and **end** of a story. What happens includes the problem and the solution.

Use information from the story Cinderella to complete the plot chart. Write what happens at the beginning, middle, and end.

Beginning

_____

_____

_____

Middle

_____

_____

_____

End

_____

_____

_____

Date: _____

Vocabulary

Word	Meaning
approximately	nearly; about
distinguish	see or hear clearly; make out plainly
erosion	being worn away little by little
feat	an achievement that shows great skill
simultaneously	at the same time
stationary	standing still; not moving
transmit	to send from one person, place, or thing to another
weightless	being free from the pull of gravity

Circle the letter next to the word that best completes each sentence.

Yesterday I went on a space walk. I spent _____ an hour

outside the station. It's hard to explain how it feels to be _____

and able to float. The weather was so clear that I could _____

a large bridge. I noticed how pollution and _____ have changed

Earth. Today, I'm going to _____ the video of my space walk

to Earth. Dad said we'll broadcast our next space walk live so our

friends everywhere on Earth can _____ see everything that we do.

1. A. happily
   B. bravely
   C. clearly
   D. approximately
2. E. weightless
   F. thankful
   G. frightened
   H. heavy

3. A. extinguish
   B. distinguish
   C. explain
   D. discover
4. E. erosion
   F. explosion
   G. emotion
   H. motion

5. A. receive
   B. tape
   C. report
   D. transmit
6. E. slowly
   F. simultaneously
   G. hardly
   H. approximately

Date: _____

Directions: Read each sentence. Write the word in the blank that best completes the sentence. Then divide the word into syllables.

1. We will have our party on _____ Day weekend.

Labor	Label

2. You might receive a ticket if you exceed the speed _____.

lemon	limit

3. The chameleon is a _____ that can change color.

ladle	lizard

4. My winning science project was pictured in the _____ newspaper.

local	level

5. Grandfather's ideas were based on _____.

logic	label

6. We played _____ tag in the park.

spinach	shadow

Fluency Focus

Sparkling Teeth

The Maya were a group of people who lived hundreds of years ago. They lived in the area that is now Central America. The Maya are famous today for their beautiful cities and their written language. They also are known to have taken great pride in their appearance. Mayan men and women often wore jewelry in their lips, noses, and ears.

Teeth were important to the Mayan people. They chewed food with their teeth, of course, but they also decorated them. Some Maya had jewels put into their teeth to improve their looks. First, a hole was drilled into a tooth. Then, a jewel was fit into the hole. The jewel could be a piece of gold, or it could be a shiny red, green, or blue stone. Getting a jewel set into one's tooth was not easy or even very safe. There was a risk of losing the tooth. One slip, and the tooth could be destroyed.

D5

Plot

A **plot** tells what happens at the **beginning, middle,** and **end** of a story. What happens includes the problem and the solution.

Use information from the story to complete the plot chart.
Write what happens at the beginning, middle, and end.

Beginning
Amanda is living on a space station with her parents.

She is feeling a little lonely.

Middle

End

Date:

Vocabulary

Homophones are words that sound the same but have different spellings and meanings.

Read each word and its meaning in the box. Then circle the correct homophone for each sentence.

D5

stationary	not moving
stationery	writing materials such as paper
feat	an achievement
feet	plural of 'foot'
wear	to have or carry on the body
ware	thing or things for sale
board	a flat piece of wood
bored	to be restless by being uninterested

1. A space station is not a _____ object.

   A. stationary

   B. stationery

2. Contacting an alien would be a great _____.

   A. feat

   B. feet

3. What kind of clothes does an alien _____?

   A. where

   B. wear

4. Sometimes Amanda gets _____ on the space station.

   A. board

   B. bored

Date:

Word Study

Directions: 1. Read the words below.
2. Identify the number of syllables.
3. Write the number in the blank next to the word.
4. Use a slash (/) to divide each word into syllables.

The first one is done for you.

1. pre / fix   2

2. divide   _____

3. closet   _____

4. reject   _____

5. broken   _____

6. polar   _____

7. rapid   _____

8. raven   _____

9. dozen   _____

10. total   _____

11. razor   _____

Fluency Focus

Sparkling Teeth

The Maya were a group of people who lived hundreds of years ago. They lived in the area that is now Central America. The Maya are famous today for their beautiful cities and their written language. They also are known to have taken great pride in their appearance. Mayan men and women often wore jewelry in their lips, noses, and ears.

Teeth were important to the Mayan people. They chewed food with their teeth, of course, but they also decorated them. Some Maya had jewels put into their teeth to improve their looks. First, a hole was drilled into a tooth. Then, a jewel was fit into the hole. The jewel could be a piece of gold, or it could be a shiny red, green, or blue stone. Getting a jewel set into one's tooth was not easy or even very safe. There was a risk of losing the tooth. One slip, and the tooth could be destroyed.

Your Turn to Write

Think about what could happen to Amanda after she communicates with the alien. Write another plot. Use the plot chart to tell what happens.

Beginning

_____

_____

_____

Middle

_____

_____

_____

End

_____

_____

_____

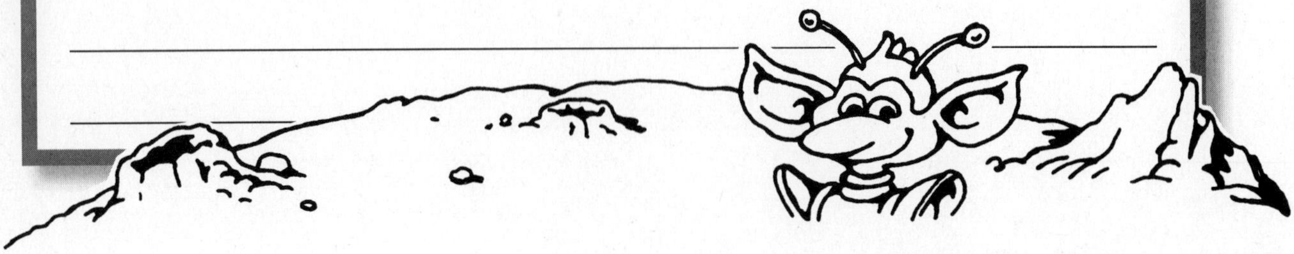

Date:

Vocabulary

D6

Directions: Draw a line to match the words to their meanings.

1. approximately

2. distinguish

3. erosion

4. feat

5. simultaneously

6. stationary

7. transmit

8. weightless

A. to send from one person, place, or thing to another

B. an achievement that shows great skill

C. at the same time

D. standing still; not moving

E. being worn away little by little

F. nearly; about

G. see or hear clearly; make out plainly

H. being free from the pull of gravity

Date: _____

Directions: Below are five definitions, each followed by a prefix or suffix. Add a root from the word box below to each prefix or suffix to make the word that matches the definition. To see how to use the word, write it in the sentence that follows.

Root	Meaning
dict	write or say
port	carry
pos	put or place
pel	push or drive
ject	throw or force

1. To carry news of something: re_____

   People who write for newspapers _____ on things that happen far away.

2. To push back: re_____

   The bug spray should _____ the mosquitoes so we won't get bitten.

3. To force in: in_____

   When you get your shot, the nurse will _____ a needle into your arm.

4. Written or spoken truth: ver_____

   The judge wanted to know the jury's _____.

Date:

Fluency Focus

Katy Allen, Future Scientist

Katy Allen sat in homeroom, waiting for the daily announcements.

"On March 20, Twain Elementary School will hold its annual Science Fair," the principal's voice boomed through the loudspeaker. "That's six weeks from now. Get busy and good luck!"

A science fair. Wow! Katy thought to herself. She imagined herself in a white coat, the kind scientists wear. She wanted to be a scientist when she grew up. And she knew exactly what she would do for her project.

Katy would build a volcano. She had read about volcanoes once in a library book of science experiments. Her volcano would be the biggest and best! It would bubble, erupt, and ooze. How cool!

She knew just how she would do it. First, she would form the volcano from clay. Then, she would put a little cup just below the opening at the top. Next, she would put baking soda and red food coloring in the cup. Last, she would add vinegar. Lava would fizz up and pour down the volcano as it erupted. Hers would be the greatest experiment ever. Katy couldn't wait to get started!

D7

Date:

Comprehension

Sequence

Writers can tell about things that happen. They write about the events in the **sequence,** or **order,** in which they happen.

Use "Goldilocks and the Three Bears" to complete the sequence chart.

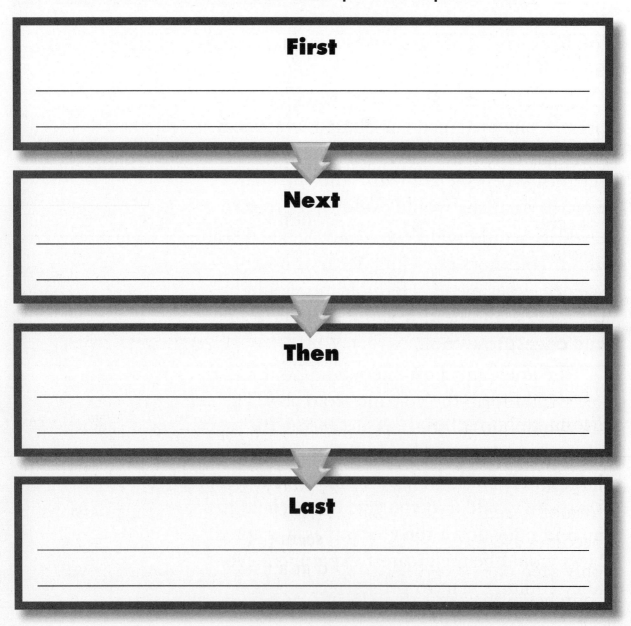

First
_____
_____

Next
_____
_____

Then
_____
_____

Last
_____
_____

Date:

Vocabulary

Word	Meaning
chrysalis	the hard cocoon, or shell, that protects a butterfly during its change from larva to adult
cluster	to stand or grow close together
emerges	comes out
habitat	the place where a plant or animal naturally lives or grows
migration	the movement of people or animals from one place to another
molt	to shed feathers, skin, hair, or shell before new growth
nectar	a sweet liquid found in many flowers
solitary	living or acting alone

Write words from the box to complete the paragraph.

chrysalis   habitat   migration   molt   nectar   solitary

The field near our house is a great summer _____ for
1
Monarch butterflies because there are milkweed plants. They can
also get _____ from the wildflowers. Last week I saw a
2
large caterpillar _____ its skin. Then I saw how it had
3
formed a _____ around itself. It won't be long before it
4
becomes a butterfly. Monarchs seem to be _____. I've
5
only seen one or two in the field at a time. The Monarchs will
soon begin their fall _____ to Mexico.
6

Date:

Word Study

Directions: For each word below, fill in the blanks with the correct prefixes and suffixes.

1. expose = _____ + pose
2. rejected = _____ + ject + ed
3. dictation = dict + _____
4. repellent = repel(l) + _____
5. portable = port + _____

Directions: Fill in the blanks with the correct meaning for each word. Use the word box at the bottom to review the meanings of the roots.

A. the act of speaking aloud
B. something that pushes away
C. to put or leave out
D. threw back
E. able to be carried

1. expose _____
2. rejected _____
3. portable _____
4. dictation _____
5. repellent _____

Root	Meaning
dict	write or say
port	carry
pos	put or place
pel	push or drive
ject	throw or force

Date:

Fluency Focus

Katy Allen, Future Scientist

Katy Allen sat in homeroom, waiting for the daily announcements.

"On March 20, Twain Elementary School will hold its annual Science Fair," the principal's voice boomed through the loudspeaker. "That's six weeks from now. Get busy and good luck!"

A science fair. Wow! Katy thought to herself. She imagined herself in a white coat, the kind scientists wear. She wanted to be a scientist when she grew up. And she knew exactly what she would do for her project.

Katy would build a volcano. She had read about volcanoes once in a library book of science experiments. Her volcano would be the biggest and best! It would bubble, erupt, and ooze. How cool!

She knew just how she would do it. First, she would form the volcano from clay. Then, she would put a little cup just below the opening at the top. Next, she would put baking soda and red food coloring in the cup. Last, she would add vinegar. Lava would fizz up and pour down the volcano as it erupted. Hers would be the greatest experiment ever. Katy couldn't wait to get started!

D8

Date:

Focus Skill

Sequence

Writers can tell about things that happen. They write about the events in the **sequence**, or **order**, in which they happen.

Use the article to complete the sequence chart. Write the migration cycle of Monarch butterflies in sequence.

Late Summer/Early Fall
Monarch butterflies begin to migrate south.
_____

Winter
_____
_____

Spring
_____
_____

Early Summer
_____
_____

Date: _____

Dictionary Skills

Dictionaries give word spellings to help the reader with pronunciations. They also give definitions of the word.

Answer the first part of each item by writing a word from the box. Answer the second part by circling the correct choice. Use the glossary to help you.

emerges	cluster	habitat	solitary

1. Write the correct spelling of (KLUSS tuhr). _____
   It means—

   a. to stand or grow close together

   b. to blow away

2. Write the correct spelling of (ee MUR jez). _____
   It means—

   a. comes out

   b. goes inside

3. Write the correct spelling of (HAB i tat). _____
   It means—

   a. the place where a plant or animal naturally lives or grows

   b. a sweet liquid found in many flowers

4. Write the correct spelling of (SOL uh ter ee). _____
   It means—

   a. to stand or grow close together

   b. living or acting alone

Directions: Read each sentence below. Underline the definition of the bolded word. Use the word box to check the meaning of the roots.

Root	Meaning
dict	write or say
port	carry
pos	put or place
pel	push or drive
ject	throw or force

1. Can someone **propose** a new game we can play?

   A. to set something in a box
   B. to put a suggestion to others
   C. to listen to others
   D. to have a talk with someone

2. The detective interviewed the suspects separately; he knew they were lying about the robbery because their stories **contradicted** one another.

   A. protect from   B. turn away from
   C. say the opposite of   D. hang over

3. The boat was **propelled** by a gas engine.

   A. sunk   B. docked
   C. pushed   D. arranged

4. A flashlight **projects** a beam of light to help you see.

   A. walks forward
   B. reaches forward
   C. bends forward
   D. throws forward

Fluency Focus

Katy Allen, Future Scientist

Katy Allen sat in homeroom, waiting for the daily announcements.

"On March 20, Twain Elementary School will hold its annual Science Fair," the principal's voice boomed through the loudspeaker. "That's six weeks from now. Get busy and good luck!"

A science fair. Wow! Katy thought to herself. She imagined herself in a white coat, the kind scientists wear. She wanted to be a scientist when she grew up. And she knew exactly what she would do for her project.

Katy would build a volcano. She had read about volcanoes once in a library book of science experiments. Her volcano would be the biggest and best! It would bubble, erupt, and ooze. How cool!

She knew just how she would do it. First, she would form the volcano from clay. Then, she would put a little cup just below the opening at the top. Next, she would put baking soda and red food coloring in the cup. Last, she would add vinegar. Lava would fizz up and pour down the volcano as it erupted. Hers would be the greatest experiment ever. Katy couldn't wait to get started!

D9

Your Turn to Write

Think about something you do that involves several steps. Then use the sequence chart below to show the steps of your routine.

First

____

____

Next

____

____

Then

____

____

Last

____

____

Vocabulary

Directions: Use what you know. Write the best word to complete each sentence.

migration	chrysalis	nectar	solitary
cluster	habitat	molt	emerges

1. As the Monarchs head south, they stop to feed on _____.

2. The _____ of the Monarch butterfly happens every year.

3. Monarchs are _____ creatures by day, but at night they _____ in groups.

4. Migration begins in late summer and early fall after each butterfly comes out of its _____.

5. After feeding on milkweed and growing quickly, the Monarch will _____ its skin several times.

6. Mexico is the perfect _____ for the Monarchs because it is cool, but not too cold.

7. The Monarch forms a chrysalis, and after about fourteen days, an adult butterfly _____.

Date:

D9

Directions: Underline the root in each word below. Then select the word from the list that makes sense in each sentence. Write the word in the blank. Use the list of roots and their meanings to help you decide which word to use.

expelled   portfolio   proposal   injecting   prediction

1. We learned how roots absorb water by _____ a stalk of celery with red ink. We *forced* the ink into the celery.

2. My art teacher wants us to keep our drawings together in a large _____ so we can *carry* them home to show our families.

3. My grandfather can make a _____ about the weather just by looking at the sky, and he almost always *says* the right thing.

4. When my family went on vacation, each of us made a _____ for a *place* to visit, and then we voted.

5. My friend was almost _____ from school for bringing his pet python to school. His pet almost *drove* him out of school.

Root	Meaning
dict	write or say
port	carry
pose	put or place
pel	push or drive
ject	throw or force

Fluency Focus

Therapy Dogs

If you were a patient in a hospital, do you think you would like a visit from a dog? Petting a warm, furry dog might cheer you up.

A therapy dog lives with a family, just like most pets. The difference is that once or twice a week, a therapy dog and its owner visit people who are sick or lonely.

A therapy dog needs to be friendly, gentle, and calm. Some young dogs can be too friendly! They need to be trained not to jump on people. Some owners take their dogs to special classes to learn how to act around young children and older people. Therapy dogs also learn to be careful around people who are using wheelchairs, crutches, and walkers.

When a dog and its owner walk through the halls of a hospital, patients smile and laugh. Therapy dogs are an instant success with most people.

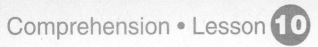

Crying thus to himself, Iktomi stepped to the water's brink. He stooped forward with a hand on each bent knee and peeped far into the deep water. "There!" he exclaimed, "I see you, my friend, sitting with your ankles wound around my little pot of fish! My friend, I am hungry. Give me a bone!"

"Ha! ha! ha!" laughed the muskrat. The sound did not rise up out of the lake, for it came down from overhead. With his hands still on his knees, Iktomi turned his face upward into the great willow tree. Opening wide his mouth he begged, "My friend, my friend, give me a bone to gnaw!"

"Ha! ha!" laughed the muskrat, and leaning over the limb he sat upon, he let fall a small sharp bone which dropped right into Iktomi's throat. Iktomi almost choked to death before he could get it out. In the tree, the muskrat sat laughing loud. "Next time, say to a visiting friend, 'Be seated beside me, my friend. Let me share with you my food.'"

Directions: Use details from "Iktomi and the Muskrat" that gave clues about what happened in the story.

What I predicted: _____

Clues that helped me predict: _____

_____

_____

What I know happened: _____

Vocabulary

Word	Meaning
anticipation	the act of looking forward to something
attentively	carefully
dismantle	to take something apart
interpret	to decide what something means
majestic	having great power and beauty
quest	a long search
significant	meaningful or important
surpassed	better, greater, or stronger than another person or thing

D10

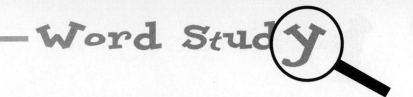

Directions: Read the following sentences. Then underline each word that has the root 'pel.'

1. Matt felt compelled to tell the teacher that he didn't have his homework.

2. A big can of bug repellent stood by the back door for everyone to use.

3. The students were expelled from the military school for cheating.

4. The propellers on small planes are so noisy that you can hardly hear anything else.

Directions: Use context clues from the sentences above to match each word to its definition. Write the letter of the correct definition on the line.

1. _____ compelled

2. _____ expelled

3. _____ propeller

4. _____ repellent

A. to be forced out of

B. felt a strong need to do something

C. something that pushes away

D. something that pushes or drives an object forward

Fluency Focus

Therapy Dogs

If you were a patient in a hospital, do you think you would like a visit from a dog? Petting a warm, furry dog might cheer you up.

A therapy dog lives with a family, just like most pets. The difference is that once or twice a week, a therapy dog and its owner visit people who are sick or lonely.

A therapy dog needs to be friendly, gentle, and calm. Some young dogs can be too friendly! They need to be trained not to jump on people. Some owners take their dogs to special classes to learn how to act around young children and older people. Therapy dogs also learn to be careful around people who are using wheelchairs, crutches, and walkers.

When a dog and its owner walk through the halls of a hospital, patients smile and laugh. Therapy dogs are an instant success with most people.

D11

Predict

Writers give clues in a story about what action or event will happen next. Story clues can help you **make predictions.**

Complete the chart. Use details from the story that gave clues about what happened in the story.

What I Predicted

Spotted Deer's fears about the sweat bath and vision quest will

not stop him.

Clues That Helped Me Predict

_____

_____

_____

_____

What I Predicted

_____

_____

Date:

Vocabulary

Directions: Read the word in the first column. Find and underline the word that has the opposite meaning.

1. **dismantle**   fix   undo   build

2. **majestic**   beautiful   unimpressive   funny

3. **excited**   upset   relaxed   encouraged

4. **vanish**   appear   disappear   depart

5. **native**   domestic   original   alien

6. **reduce**   magnify   lessen   redo

7. **identical**   identity   similar   different

8. **foreign**   unknown   native   amusing

D11

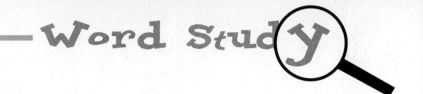
Directions: Underline each word with the root 'pos.' Each underlined word matches one of the clues for the crossword puzzle.

1. Karl promised that he wouldn't impose on his father's work time again.

2. In ballet class, Eva learned how to hold her feet in fifth position.

3. Dad makes a deposit at the bank every time he gets paid.

4. Recycling is the best way to dispose of plastic and paper.

5. Jody will compose a letter to her pen pal in Hong Kong.

6. When he was studying photography, Lamar learned never to expose film to light.

7. Mrs. Gardner proposed paying Marcus ten dollars for mowing her lawn.

Down:
2. put forward, suggested
3. totally different
5. to place responsibility on
8. a place, location

Across:
1. to put away, get rid of
4. put out, uncover
6. create or write
7. to put money in the bank

Date:

Fluency Focus

Therapy Dogs

If you were a patient in a hospital, do you think you would like a visit from a dog? Petting a warm, furry dog might cheer you up.

A therapy dog lives with a family, just like most pets. The difference is that once or twice a week, a therapy dog and its owner visit people who are sick or lonely.

A therapy dog needs to be friendly, gentle, and calm. Some young dogs can be too friendly! They need to be trained not to jump on people. Some owners take their dogs to special classes to learn how to act around young children and older people. Therapy dogs also learn to be careful around people who are using wheelchairs, crutches, and walkers.

When a dog and its owner walk through the halls of a hospital, patients smile and laugh. Therapy dogs are an instant success with most people.

Date:

Your Turn to Write

Think of a challenge you have faced in your life. Use the chart to plan a story that tells about how you overcame the challenge.

Prediction Readers Should Make

_____

_____

Clues That Help the Reader Predict

_____

_____

_____

_____

What Happened

_____

_____

Date:

Vocabulary

Circle the letter next to the word that best completes each sentence.

1. As a boy, Spotted Deer _____ others with his skills.
   A. surpassed
   B. surrounded
   C. survived
   D. celebrated

2. Spotted Deer tried to calm his fears in _____ of the sweat bath.
   E. admiration
   F. appreciation
   G. imitation
   H. anticipation

3. Instead of crying out, he listened _____ to the elders' songs.
   A. hurriedly
   B. lazily
   C. attentively
   D. unhappily

4. Spotted Deer was ready for his *hanblechia*, the most _____ event in his life.
   E. unimportant
   F. significant
   G. amusing
   H. disappointing

5. During the vision _____, he would ask for strength.
   A. month
   B. question
   C. examination
   D. quest

6. After his *hanblechia*, an elder would _____ Spotted Deer's dreams.
   E. interrupt
   F. interpret
   G. invent
   H. ignore

D12

Directions: Look at the list of words below. Put a circle around all of the words that are compound words.

1. airline
2. playing
3. toothbrush
4. slipcover
5. hanger
6. rainbow
7. tiptoe
8. snowing
9. baseball
10. buttercup

Directions: For the following compound words, draw a line between the two smaller words. The first one is done for you.

1. air / mail	2. payoff
3. spotlight	4. trashcan
5. lookout	6. clipboard
7. scrapbook	8. washcloth
9. sidewalk	10. eyeball
11. streetcar	12. headlight
13. cupcake	14. broadcast
15. breakfast	16. tugboat
17. campfire	18. shoelace

Date:

Fluency Focus

Say "Dinosaur"

The Chang family was having fun singing along with their car radio. They were on summer vacation, and they were driving to Fossil River National Park.

Mr. Chang suddenly announced, "Hey, look everyone. There's a dinosaur ahead."

Terrence quickly leaned forward in the backseat and shouted, "Where?"

Mr. Chang pointed, "Just ahead. Right next to the road. See it?" He slowed the car as they approached a gigantic green dinosaur at the edge of the highway.

"It's not just *any* dinosaur. It's an *Apatosaurus*!" Terrence shouted. "There's no need to fear, though. It's an herbivore, so it only eats plants."

Kristy rolled her eyes. "It's not a real dinosaur, Dad," she said.

Mrs. Chang looked back at her son. "Terrence, I'm always amazed at how much you know about dinosaurs."

The dinosaur had a welcoming smile painted onto its face.

"Can we take a picture, Daddy?" Kristy asked.

"Sure," Mr. Chang answered.

The family got out of the car and Mr. Chang, Terrence, and Kristy lined up in front of the dinosaur. Mrs. Chang stood before them with the camera. She said, "Say 'dinosaur.'"

"Dinosaur!" everyone shouted. The camera clicked.

D13

Comprehension

Compare and Contrast

Writers **compare** to show how two or more things are alike. They **contrast** to show how the things are different.

Directions: Fill in the diagram. Under the name of each animal classification, write details that tell about that animal. Under 'Both,' write details that tell about both animal classifications.

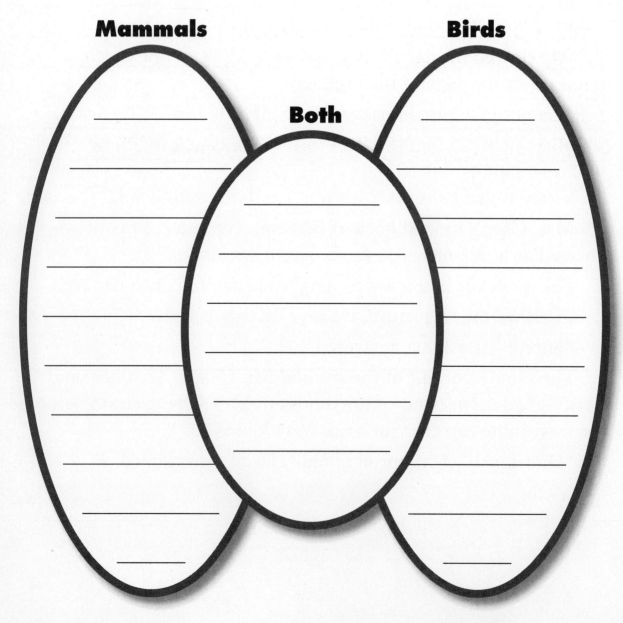

Mammals

Birds

Both

Date:

Vocabulary

Directions: Read each word and its definition below.

Word	Definition
conventional	usual
developer	one who builds something or makes something grow
edible	able to be eaten
incorporating	making a part of
inspiration	a sudden bright idea
palate	the sense of taste
savory	pleasing in taste or smell
stylist	one who arranges or designs something

D13

Directions: For the following words, circle the two smaller words that are used in each compound word.

1. playpen

| pen | lay | pin | plane | play | pan |

2. yourself

| your | our | self | elf | you | ours |

3. snowflake

| now | flake | snow | owl | lake | wake |

4. steamboat

| team | boat | steam | oat | am | at |

5. broomstick

| broom | tick | rooms | stick | brick | trick |

6. handshake

| and | sand | hand | shake | hands | hike |

7. campground

| am | ground | camp | round | ramp | noun |

8. haystack

| hays | tack | stay | hay | stick | stack |

9. sweatshirt

| wheat | eat | sweat | hurt | shirt | sweet |

Bonus Activity: Create new compound words using the words in the boxes above.

Fluency Focus

Say "Dinosaur"

The Chang family was having fun singing along with their car radio. They were on summer vacation, and they were driving to Fossil River National Park.

Mr. Chang suddenly announced, "Hey, look everyone. There's a dinosaur ahead."

Terrence quickly leaned forward in the backseat and shouted, "Where?"

Mr. Chang pointed, "Just ahead. Right next to the road. See it?" He slowed the car as they approached a gigantic green dinosaur at the edge of the highway.

"It's not just *any* dinosaur. It's an *Apatosaurus*!" Terrence shouted. "There's no need to fear, though. It's an herbivore, so it only eats plants."

Kristy rolled her eyes. "It's not a real dinosaur, Dad," she said.

Mrs. Chang looked back at her son. "Terrence, I'm always amazed at how much you know about dinosaurs."

The dinosaur had a welcoming smile painted onto its face.

"Can we take a picture, Daddy?" Kristy asked.

"Sure," Mr. Chang answered.

The family got out of the car and Mr. Chang, Terrence, and Kristy lined up in front of the dinosaur. Mrs. Chang stood before them with the camera. She said, "Say 'dinosaur.'"

"Dinosaur!" everyone shouted. The camera clicked.

D14

Compare and Contrast

Use the article to fill in the diagram. Under the name of each job, write details that tell about that job. Under 'Both,' write details that tell about both jobs.

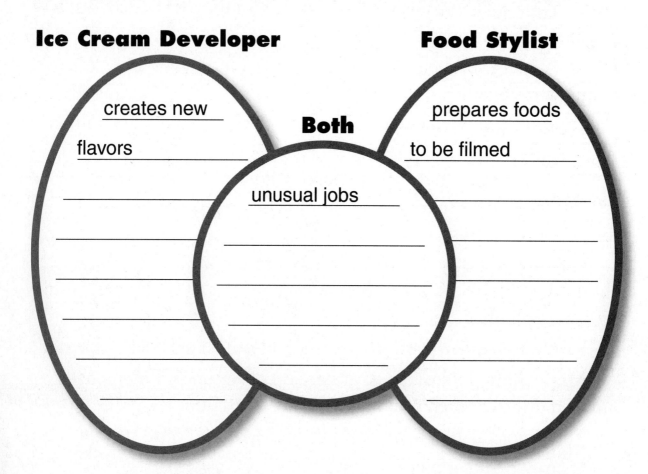

Ice Cream Developer

creates new

flavors

Both

unusual jobs

Food Stylist

prepares foods

to be filmed

Date:

Vocabulary

Word	Definition
conventional	usual
developer	one who builds something or makes something grow
edible	able to be eaten
incorporating	making a part of
inspiration	a sudden bright idea
palate	the sense of taste
savory	pleasing in taste or smell
stylist	one who arranges or designs something

Write words from the box to complete the paragraphs.

conventional   edible   incorporating
inspiration   palate   savory

Many insects are _____ and some people enjoy eating them. Eating a lollipop with a cricket in the center is not my idea of something _____ . I would definitely want to clean my _____ after tasting that!

Until recently, insects have not been a part of the _____ American diet. Now, some chefs are finding that insects give them _____ for new dishes. However, it will still be a long time before I think about _____ fried mealworms into my diet!

D14

Date:

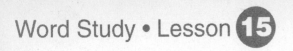

Directions: Divide each compound word in the word box, and
then fill in the blanks with a word from the word box.

| driftwood | waterfront | cardboard | junkyard | sunburn |
| beanstalk | quicksand | textbook | landmark | gingerbread |

1. Tim got a bad _____ at the beach.

2. That box is made of _____.

3. Don't step on the _____ or you'll sink.

4. For today's assignment, you need your English _____.

5. Pieces of _____ floated to the shore.

6. The house was on the _____ with a view of the sea.

7. Mrs. Lee made _____ cookies for dessert.

8. In the story, Jack climbed up a _____.

9. There are a lot of old cars at the _____.

10. That building is a _____ because of what happened
    there.

Bonus Activity: Write two sentences using words from the word
box above.

138   Lesson D15   Date:

Fluency Focus

Say "Dinosaur"

The Chang family was having fun singing along with their car radio. They were on summer vacation, and they were driving to Fossil River National Park.

Mr. Chang suddenly announced, "Hey, look everyone. There's a dinosaur ahead."

Terrence quickly leaned forward in the backseat and shouted, "Where?"

Mr. Chang pointed, "Just ahead. Right next to the road. See it?" He slowed the car as they approached a gigantic green dinosaur at the edge of the highway.

"It's not just *any* dinosaur. It's an *Apatosaurus*!" Terrence shouted. "There's no need to fear, though. It's an herbivore, so it only eats plants."

Kristy rolled her eyes. "It's not a real dinosaur, Dad," she said.

Mrs. Chang looked back at her son. "Terrence, I'm always amazed at how much you know about dinosaurs."

The dinosaur had a welcoming smile painted onto its face.

"Can we take a picture, Daddy?" Kristy asked.

"Sure," Mr. Chang answered.

The family got out of the car and Mr. Chang, Terrence, and Kristy lined up in front of the dinosaur. Mrs. Chang stood before them with the camera. She said, "Say 'dinosaur.'"

"Dinosaur!" everyone shouted. The camera clicked.

D15

Your Turn to Write

Directions: Choose a job from the article. Then choose another job you know about. Use the diagram to compare and contrast the two jobs.

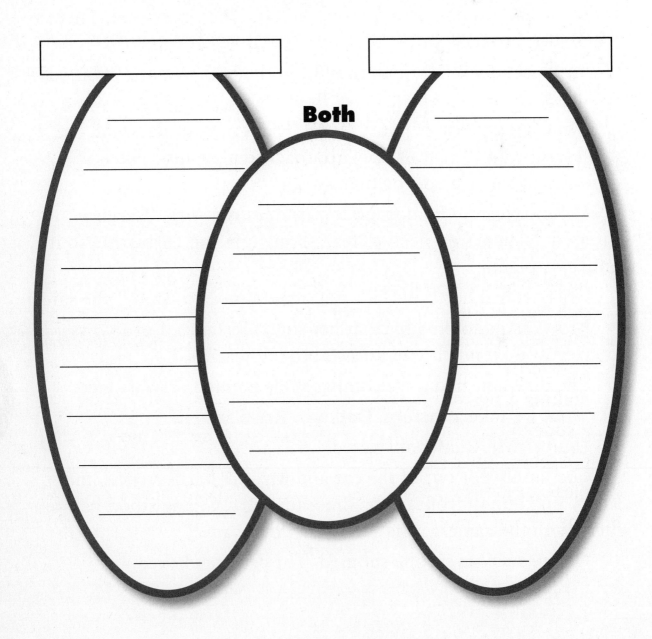

Both

Date:

Vocabulary

Directions: Read the clues below. Match the clue to the words, then find and circle each word in the puzzle.

```
c s t y l i s t a p t x n t u o n r l m f
e w a f u v t y g h d e v e l o p e r k u
d q h t y j s n y o m g z h m b a b w s m
i n s p i r a t i o n a s a x o l f d a e
b w z s p d p j k v e p m t q s a d c v e
l p c o n v e n t i o n a l c k t b w o g
e d x b a y w b m z e m t d p g e v t r t
v m i n c o r p o r a t i n g i r c p y h
```

1. usual or ordinary _____
2. one who builds something or makes something grow _____
3. able to be eaten _____
4. making a part of _____
5. a sudden bright idea _____
6. the sense of taste _____
7. pleasing in taste or smell _____
8. one who arranges or designs something _____

D15

Directions: Read each incomplete word below and the meaning that follows. Write the correct prefix to complete the word on the line. The first one is done for you.

Prefix	Meaning
uni-	one
bi-	two
tri-	three
multi-	many or much
semi-	half or partly
pre-	before
pro-	forward

1. __bi__ plane (an airplane with two sets of wings)

2. _____ view (to view something before anyone else)

3. _____ cycle (a vehicle with one wheel)

4. _____ dry (partly dry)

5. _____ cooked (cooked before)

6. _____ cycle (a vehicle with three wheels)

Date:

Fluency Focus

Cut Out the Knives

Not everyone eats with forks, knives, and spoons. Some people eat with chopsticks. Chopsticks are a pair of long, thin sticks used for eating solid food. They are mainly used in Asian countries. The custom of using chopsticks began in China long ago when there was a low supply of cooking fuel. To use less fuel, the Chinese people cut their food into little pieces before cooking it. Food that was cut into small pieces cooked faster than food that remained in large pieces. Food was then served in bite-sized bits, so knives were no longer needed at meals. Chopsticks took their place at the table, helping people pick up food bite by bite. Today, most chopsticks are made of wood or bamboo, but they can also be made of ivory, jade, silver, or even gold. Have you ever used chopsticks? Give them a try!

D16

Date:

Comprehension

Inference

Readers use story clues and what they already know to **make inferences** about characters and events.

Complete the chart. Use details from the story to support the inference.

Inference
_____
_____

Supporting Detail
_____
_____

Supporting Detail
_____
_____

Date: _____

Word	Meaning
accustomed	in the habit of doing something
affectionately	in an affectionate or loving way
bleachers	raised seats or benches arranged in rows for better viewing of an event
determined	having made a firm decision; showing the ability to stick to a purpose
intently	in a purposeful or intent way
knowingly	in a knowing way; with understanding
objected	disliked or disagreed
scrimmage	a game played for practice in sports

D16

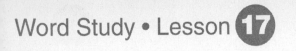

Directions: Underline the prefix in each word below.

1. uniform	6. preschool
2. trifold	7. multilevel
3. prepaid	8. semisweet
4. unicycle	9. multicolor
5. triceps	10. semiannual

Directions: Read each sentence below. Complete the sentence by adding a prefix from the list below to the bolded word. Write the new word on the line.

Prefix	Meaning
uni-	one
bi-	two
tri-	three
multi-	many or much
semi-	half or partly
pre-	before
pro-	forward

1. Before kindergarten, Jamal went to _____. (**school**)

2. The building has six levels. It is a _____ building. (**level**)

3. Sam likes to ride his _____ because it has one wheel. (**cycle**)

4. Rica _____ for his movie tickets beforehand because he knew they would sell out. (**paid**)

5. Huck's Store is having its _____ sale that it has every half of year. (**annual**)

Date:

Fluency Focus

Cut Out the Knives

Not everyone eats with forks, knives, and spoons. Some people eat with chopsticks. Chopsticks are a pair of long, thin sticks used for eating solid food. They are mainly used in Asian countries. The custom of using chopsticks began in China long ago when there was a low supply of cooking fuel. To use less fuel, the Chinese people cut their food into little pieces before cooking it. Food that was cut into small pieces cooked faster than food that remained in large pieces. Food was then served in bite-sized bits, so knives were no longer needed at meals. Chopsticks took their place at the table, helping people pick up food bite by bite. Today, most chopsticks are made of wood or bamboo, but they can also be made of ivory, jade, silver, or even gold. Have you ever used chopsticks? Give them a try!

D17

Inference

Readers use story clues and what they already know to **make inferences** about characters and events.

Complete the chart. Use details from the story to support the inference.

Inference

_____

_____

Supporting Detail

_____

_____

Supporting Detail

_____

_____

Date:

Vocabulary

Directions: Fill in the circle next to the word that completes each sentence.

Years ago, girls just didn't play football. Now we are
_____ to seeing girls participate in almost all sports.
1

Teresa was _____ to follow her dream. Although Teresa's
2

brother _____, she joined a football league. Now, instead
3

of sitting in the _____, she's playing. Her team won the
4

first _____ thanks to Teresa!
5

1. Ⓐ awakened
   Ⓑ limited
   Ⓒ confused
   Ⓓ accustomed

3. Ⓐ objected
   Ⓑ offered
   Ⓒ planned
   Ⓓ protected

5. Ⓐ field
   Ⓑ scramble
   Ⓒ scrimmage
   Ⓓ race

2. Ⓔ disturbed
   Ⓕ discovered
   Ⓖ delicious
   Ⓗ determined

4. Ⓔ bleaches
   Ⓕ bleachers
   Ⓖ dark
   Ⓗ office

D17

Directions: Read each sentence below. Circle the prefix that makes the bolded word complete.

1. Keesha bought a ___ **owned** car instead of a new one.
   - A. uni- (one)
   - B. tri- (three)
   - C. pre- (before)
   - D. multi- (many *or* much)

2. In a private school, everyone wears the same ___ **form.**
   - A. uni- (one)
   - B. multi- (many *or* much)
   - C. bi- (two)
   - D. semi- (half *or* partly)

3. Elena got a vehicle with three wheels today. Elena got a ___**cycle** today.
   - A. pre- (before)
   - B. tri- (three)
   - C. semi- (half *or* partly)
   - D. pro- (before *or* forward)

4. Martina gets a paycheck twice a month. Martina gets paid ___**weekly.**
   - A. uni- (one)
   - B. pre- (before)
   - C. multi- (many *or* much)
   - D. bi- (two)

5. The paint on the wall is partly shiny. The paint on the wall has a ___**gloss.**
   - A. bi- (two)
   - B. tri- (three)
   - C. semi- (half *or* partly)
   - D. pro- (before *or* forward)

Fluency Focus

Cut Out the Knives

Not everyone eats with forks, knives, and spoons. Some people eat with chopsticks. Chopsticks are a pair of long, thin sticks used for eating solid food. They are mainly used in Asian countries. The custom of using chopsticks began in China long ago when there was a low supply of cooking fuel. To use less fuel, the Chinese people cut their food into little pieces before cooking it. Food that was cut into small pieces cooked faster than food that remained in large pieces. Food was then served in bite-sized bits, so knives were no longer needed at meals. Chopsticks took their place at the table, helping people pick up food bite by bite. Today, most chopsticks are made of wood or bamboo, but they can also be made of ivory, jade, silver, or even gold. Have you ever used chopsticks? Give them a try!

D18

Date: _____

Your Turn to Write

Imagine a character who is really good at something, such as a subject in school or a special talent. Use the chart to plan a story.

Inference I Want Readers to Make

_____

_____

Supporting Detail

_____

_____

_____

Supporting Detail

_____

_____

_____

Date:

Vocabulary

Directions: Read each question. Circle the best answer.

| objected | intently | scrimmage | affectionately |
| knowingly | accustomed | bleachers | determined |

1. Which word also means "disliked or disagreed"?
   a. objected   b. knowingly

2. Which word is a synonym for "purposefully"?
   a. knowingly   b. intently

3. What is a "scrimmage"?
   a. a raised seat   b. a practice game

4. Which word is an antonym for "in an unloving way"?
   a. affectionately   b. intently

5. Which word means "with understanding"?
   a. knowingly   b. affectionately

6. If you are in the habit of doing something, you are _____ to doing it.
   a. determined   b. accustomed

7. What are raised seats or benches arranged in rows called?
   a. scrimmage   b. bleachers

D18

8. If you show an ability to stick to a purpose, you are _____.
   a. accustomed   b. determined

Date: _____

Directions: Underline the suffix in each word below. Use the chart to help you identify the suffixes.

Suffix	Meaning
-er/-or	someone or something that does the action
-en	made of, to make, or become
-ward	in the direction of
-fy	to make into or similar to
-less	without
-ness	state or quality of

1. sleepless   3. madness   5. doctor

2. weaken   4. northward   6. falsify

Directions: Fill in the blanks below to create a word to match each definition. Write the correct suffix on the first blank line and the new word on the second blank line. Use the chart above and spelling rules below to help you.

Spelling Rules:
- If a root word ends in 'e,' just add 'r' when adding the suffix '-er' or '-or.'
- If the root word ends in 'e,' change the 'e' to an 'i' and add 'fy' when adding the suffix '-fy.'
- If the root word ends in 'y,' change the 'y' to an 'i' when adding the suffix '-less' or '-ness.'

1. drive + _____ = _____ (one who drives)

2. sleep + _____ = _____ (without sleep)

3. north + _____ = _____ (in the direction of north)

Fluency Focus

Chicago Saturday

Towering skyscrapers, honking cars, roaring trains, fluttering pigeons—that's Chicago. Simon loved it all. It was his home. And today was Saturday, Simon's favorite day. His big brother, Jerry, was taking him to the museum.

The boys took the train to State Street and walked toward the Field Museum of Natural History. Simon stopped to look back at the city's skyscrapers. "They really do look like they're scraping the sky," he said out loud.

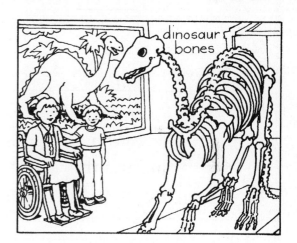

dinosaur bones

Simon and Jerry had seen the dinosaur skeletons at this museum many times. But it was always fun to take another look. Simon especially liked the statues of the first cave people, even though most of them looked pretty scary.

Jerry talked Simon into touring a tomb from ancient Egypt. Then they went through several rooms filled with insects. Simon stopped to look at a case filled with glittering beetles.

The boys made a last stop to look at meteorites that had fallen to Earth from outer space. There was so much to see at the museum that they could have

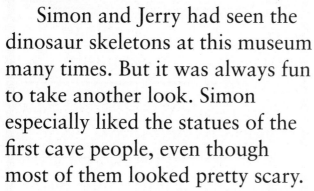

stayed all day. But they had to get back home for lunch. Dad was making his famous Chicago-style hot dogs with "the works."

D19

Date:

155

Comprehension

Directions: Use the chart to list the facts and opinions from the article.

Facts About Hummingbirds	Opinions About Hummingbirds
1. _____ _____ _____ _____	1. _____ _____ _____ _____
2. _____ _____ _____ _____	2. _____ _____ _____ _____
3. _____ _____ _____ _____	3. _____ _____ _____ _____
4. _____ _____ _____ _____	4. _____ _____ _____ _____

Date:

Vocabulary

Directions: Draw a line connecting each vocabulary word on the left with its correct definition on the right.

conservation   an animal that is hunted

fisheries   noticed

observed   a living thing that is hurt

perish   suffering from hunger

population   protection of wildlife

prey   die

starvation   a group living in one place

victim   where fish are raised

Directions: Underline the suffix in each word below. Use the chart to help you identify the suffixes.

Suffix	Meaning
-er/-or	someone or something that does the action
-en	made of, to make, or become
-ward	in the direction of
-fy	to make into or similar to
-less	without
-ness	state or quality of

1. wooden
2. satisfy
3. writer
4. toward
5. careless
6. sadness

Directions: Form a new word by putting together the root word and suffix. Use the spelling rules to help you.

Spelling Rules:
- If a root word ends in 'e,' just add 'r' when adding the suffix '-er' or '-or.'
- If the root word ends in 'e,' change the 'e' to an 'i' and add 'fy' when adding the suffix '-fy.'
- If the root word ends in 'y,' change the 'y' to an 'i' when adding the suffix '-less' or '-ness.'

1. west (direction or location) + -ward (in the direction of)

   = _____ (in the direction of west)

2. sad (a feeling) + -ness (state or quality of) = _____
   (state of feeling sad)

Fluency Focus

Chicago Saturday

Towering skyscrapers, honking cars, roaring trains, fluttering pigeons—that's Chicago. Simon loved it all. It was his home. And today was Saturday, Simon's favorite day. His big brother, Jerry, was taking him to the museum.

The boys took the train to State Street and walked toward the Field Museum of Natural History. Simon stopped to look back at the city's skyscrapers. "They really do look like they're scraping the sky," he said out loud.

dinosaur bones

Simon and Jerry had seen the dinosaur skeletons at this museum many times. But it was always fun to take another look. Simon especially liked the statues of the first cave people, even though most of them looked pretty scary.

Jerry talked Simon into touring a tomb from ancient Egypt. Then they went through several rooms filled with insects. Simon stopped to look at a case filled with glittering beetles.

The boys made a last stop to look at meteorites that had fallen to Earth from outer space. There was so much to see at the museum that they could have

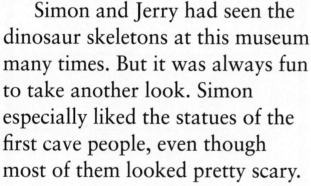

stayed all day. But they had to get back home for lunch. Dad was making his famous Chicago-style hot dogs with "the works."

D20

Fact and Opinion

A **fact** is something that can be proven. An **opinion** is a person's belief or feeling.

Use the chart to list the facts and opinions you find in the article.

Facts About Sharks	Scientists' Opinions
1. When a shark attacks a human, it takes one bite and swims away.	1. Sharks don't like the taste of humans.
2. _____	2. _____
3. _____	3. _____

Tell if each sentence is a fact or an opinion. Explain your answer.

4. There are about fifty shark attacks around the world in one year.

_____

_____

5. The number of shark attacks is reason enough to kill sharks.

_____

_____

Date:

Vocabulary

Choose words from the box to complete the paragraph. Write the correct word on each line.

| fisheries |
| observed |
| perish |
| population |
| prey |
| victim |

Are you afraid that you will be the _____ of a shark attack? Don't
1
worry. Many scientists have _____
2
that sharks actually prefer to eat mammals like
seals and sea lions. Other _____
3
include octopuses and fish. Some scientists think
it is not a good idea to let sharks _____. They believe
4
that the _____ of seals and sea lions would increase,
5
which would destroy the balance of nature. Also, more lobster
_____ would continue to be invaded by octopuses.
6

Extend Your Vocabulary

<u>Suffixes</u> A suffix is a word part that is added to the end of a word.
A suffix changes the meaning of the base word.

**Fill in the blank spaces in the chart. Be sure to spell the
vocabulary words correctly.**

7.

to protect	+ the act of	= the act of protecting
conserve	+ ation	= _____

8.

to suffer from hunger	+ the state of	= the state of suffering from hunger
starve	+ ation	= _____

D20

Part A

superman	superstar	supermarket	supervisor
supersonic	subway	suburban	subtitle
subsoil	subculture	subtotal	subplot

Part B

Directions: Draw a line from each word in the left-hand column to its definition, which is located somewhere in the right-hand column.

superman   a man above other men

superstar   a market whose size is over that of a small
                                      market or grocery store

supermarket   part of a culture that's below or inside of the
                                      larger culture

supervisor   a total below or part of the larger total

supersonic   above the regular speed of sound

subway   ground that is below the top layer of soil

suburban   a person who is more than or above a regular
                                      star

subtitle   a title written below or after the first title

subsoil   a person who oversees another person's work

subculture   a story plot that is below or inside of the
                                      larger plot

subtotal   a path that runs below ground

subplot   the area outside of a city where there are
                                      fewer people than in the city

Fluency Focus

The Story of Salt and Pepper

Today salt and pepper are readily available, and many people add them to their food. But these popular seasonings have not always been available to everyone. In ancient times, salt and pepper were very precious and were sometimes exchanged for other goods.

Salt was produced in the center of the Sahara, the largest desert in the world. Traders used camel caravans to carry heavy loads of salt to West Africa, where the salt was traded for gold and other goods. In many areas around the Mediterranean Sea, cakes of salt were used as money.

Pepper was a very popular and valuable spice in the Roman Empire. A single peppercorn dropped on the floor was hunted like a lost pearl. The main street of Rome's spice market was called "Pepper Street." When the Roman Empire fell, the supply of pepper and many other spices dried up in Europe.

Date:

Directions: After listening to the passage, write the main idea in the large box and write the supporting details in the circles.

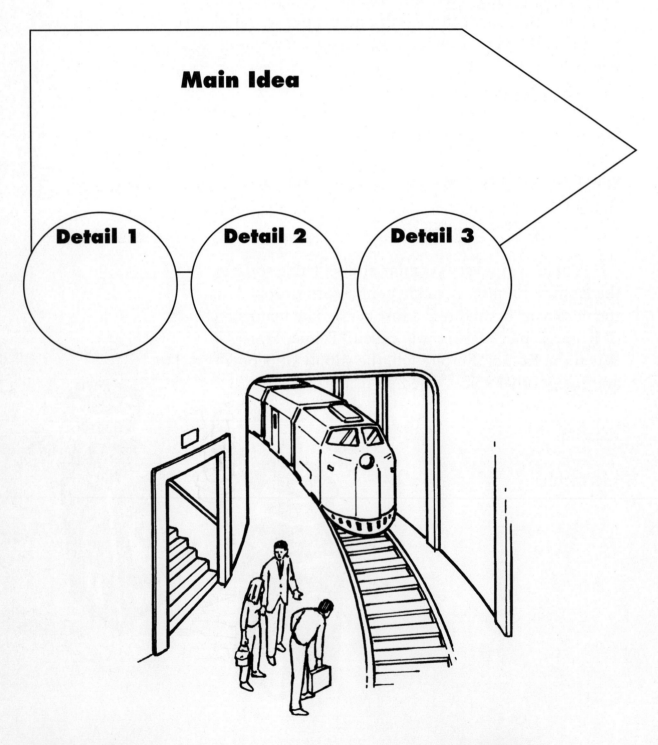

Main Idea

Detail 1

Detail 2

Detail 3

Date:

Directions: Look at the list of words below and use those words to answer the questions. Hint: You will not be using two of the words.

Which words name things you would find inside a cave?

_____ _____ _____

What words might describe those things?

_____ _____ _____

What words might describe someone who goes into caves a lot to study things they find there so that we can learn more about them?

_____ _____

chambers   fragile

enthusiastic   descent

stalactites   unique

reliable   spelunking

spectacular   stalagmites

Directions: Read each of the definitions below. Also read the words that follow the definitions. Attach a prefix to the word that will help it to mean the same as the definition. Choose from the prefix 'sub-' or 'super-.'

Definition: **Word:**

a topic that is under or inside of the main topic   _____topic

a hero greater than normal heroes   _____hero

a level underneath of the top level   _____level

qualities that are over and above what is natural   _____natural

below standard expectations   _____standard

over or above what is human   _____human

a set that is inside of another one   _____set

used below the water level   _____marine

Fluency Focus

The Story of Salt and Pepper

Today salt and pepper are readily available, and many people add them to their food. But these popular seasonings have not always been available to everyone. In ancient times, salt and pepper were very precious and were sometimes exchanged for other goods.

Salt was produced in the center of the Sahara, the largest desert in the world. Traders used camel caravans to carry heavy loads of salt to West Africa, where the salt was traded for gold and other goods. In many areas around the Mediterranean Sea, cakes of salt were used as money.

Pepper was a very popular and valuable spice in the Roman Empire. A single peppercorn dropped on the floor was hunted like a lost pearl. The main street of Rome's spice market was called "Pepper Street." When the Roman Empire fell, the supply of pepper and many other spices dried up in Europe.

Date:

Main Idea and Supporting Details

The **main idea** is the most important idea of an article. Writers use **supporting details** to tell more about the main idea. A paragraph may also have its own main idea and supporting details.

Use the information from the article to fill in the main idea chart.

Main Idea

Spelunking allows people to see the many wonders of caves.

Supporting Detail	**Supporting Detail**	**Supporting Detail**
_____	_____	_____
_____	_____	_____
_____	_____	_____
_____	_____	_____

Directions: Draw a line from the each word in the left-hand column to its definition, which is located somewhere in the right-hand column.

chambers   thin pieces of rock that hang down
                                            from the roof of a cave

enthusiastic   the hobby of exploring caves

stalactites   one of a kind

reliable   delicate or easily broken

spectacular   movement from a higher place to a
                                            lower one

fragile   thin pieces of rock that stick up
                                            from the floor of a cave

descent   large rooms

unique   excited or full of interest

spelunking   remarkable or amazing

stalagmites   can be depended on

Directions: Read the passage. While reading, circle each word containing the prefix sub- or the prefix super-. Below the passage, write each word you find in the word column. Define each word in the space next to it, on the right.

Some people are scared to ride the subway, but for others, the subway is fun to ride. Subways are found in cities, not in suburbs, because there are so many city people who need to ride the subway. They take the subway to school, to work, to events, to the doctor, and even to the supermarket — unless they buy too many groceries. The train conductor supervises the people on the subway cars and is the person to contact if there is an emergency. With so many riders, there is a great subculture on the subway train. Just look at the faces around you!

Word: **Definition:**

_____   _____

_____   _____

_____   _____

_____   _____

_____   _____

Fluency Focus

The Story of Salt and Pepper

Today salt and pepper are readily available, and many people add them to their food. But these popular seasonings have not always been available to everyone. In ancient times, salt and pepper were very precious and were sometimes exchanged for other goods.

Salt was produced in the center of the Sahara, the largest desert in the world. Traders used camel caravans to carry heavy loads of salt to West Africa, where the salt was traded for gold and other goods. In many areas around the Mediterranean Sea, cakes of salt were used as money.

Pepper was a very popular and valuable spice in the Roman Empire. A single peppercorn dropped on the floor was hunted like a lost pearl. The main street of Rome's spice market was called "Pepper Street." When the Roman Empire fell, the supply of pepper and many other spices dried up in Europe.

Your Turn to Write

Think about an outdoor activity that you enjoy. What training or equipment do you need? What can you see or learn? Use the chart to write the main idea and supporting details about the activity.

Main Idea

_____

Supporting Detail

_____

_____

_____

_____

Supporting Detail

_____

_____

_____

_____

Supporting Detail

_____

_____

_____

_____

Date: _____

Vocabulary

Read each sentence. Circle the best meaning for the underlined word.

1. This cave is full of tunnels and <u>chambers</u> to explore.

   holes   large rooms   long ropes

2. Make your <u>descent</u> by placing each foot lower on the ladder.

   upward climb   downward climb   sideways climb

3. Caves may contain <u>unique</u> life forms not seen anywhere else.

   very common   dangerous   one of a kind

4. Prepare to see <u>spectacular</u> rock shapes the next time you go caving.

   ordinary   striped   amazing

5. Spelunkers are <u>enthusiastic</u> about caving.

   nervous   uninformed   excited

6. It is important to use <u>reliable</u> equipment when you go caving.

   dependable   interesting   strange

7. You must be careful in a cave because the rock shapes can be <u>fragile</u>.

   easily broken   strong   surprising

Dictionary Skills: Dictionaries give word spellings to help you with pronunciations. They also give definitions. Write the correct word from the box. Then write the word's meaning.

8. (stuh LAK tyts) _____

   _____

9. (spee LUNG king) _____

   _____

10. (stuh LAG myts) _____

   _____

spelunking
stalactites
stalagmites

Directions: Choose the prefix that will make each word match the definition. Write the prefix in the blank space before the word.

sub	super	over	under

Word	Definition

1. _____ cooked — cooked too much

2. _____ shirt — a shirt worn under another one

3. _____ set — a set of numbers, letters, etc. contained within a larger set

4. _____ ground — below or underneath ground level

5. _____ impose — to impose or place something over or above something else

6. _____ hand — thrown with the hand above or over the shoulder

7. _____ natural — above or beyond what is natural

8. _____ way — an underground way or passage; an underground railway

9. _____ draw — take money from a bank account that is over the amount available

10. _____ value — to value less than what is necessary

Fluency Focus

Fascinating Bats

Can you imagine a cave full of bats? Tens of thousands of them sometimes live together in one cave! Bats can live in caves, trees, deserts, and even in house attics.

Over the years, bats have had some bad press, especially in horror movies. But bats do not attack humans or get caught in people's hair. Bats are not vicious. In fact, bats are good for the environment. Most cave-dwelling bats eat tons of crop-destroying insects.

Bats are active at night and they rest during the day. How do bats get around in the dark of night? They use their excellent sense of hearing. Most bats can actually see very well, but eyesight is of little use in the dark, so many bats "see" by listening to echoes.

A bat makes high-pitched sounds that bounce off objects around it. The bat listens to the echoes and is able to judge how far away an object is, its size, and if it is moving.

Date:

Comprehension

Directions: Read the passage below. Pay close attention to the characters Marco and Mami. What can you learn about them based on what they do, say, think, and feel, as well as from details that the author provides about them? Fill out the chart below the passage with what you have learned about Marco and Mami.

On Monday, Marco felt like he woke up on the wrong side of the bed. Not only did he oversleep, but the Florida sky, which was normally a bright blue, was overcast. Marco's Mami yelled that if he didn't hurry up, he would be late and would miss the bus again. Plus, Mami would be late to work and wouldn't be paid overtime. "Marco! Why did you oversleep?" Mami yelled from the kitchen, while Marco still lay in bed in his undershirt and pajama pants. Marco yelled back, "I couldn't tell what time it was, Mami." He blamed it on the dark grey cloud that rested overtop of their house and covered up the sun. Mami opened Marco's door and laughed, saying, "Marco, my boy, I won't underestimate you. You know how to read the clock. Now get out of bed."

MARCO	MAMI

Vocabulary

1. cantaloupe—What does a cantaloupe look like? You can compare it to something else if that would help you describe it.

2. ingredients—What are some ingredients that you might put in a fruit salad?

3. generous

4. expression—Use your face to make a funny or confused expression.

5. doubtful

6. spewed

7. anxious

8. nudging

9. affectionately—What type of pet do you think acts the most affectionately—a dog or a cat? Explain why.

10. complicate—Does following instructions help or complicate things when you are taking a test?

Date:

Directions: Draw a line from each word in the left-hand column to its definition, which is located somewhere in the right-hand column.

Words

Definitions

overburden

a student who is under the level of graduating

oversight

to flow over or beyond the limit of something

undercover

spying under protection so as not to be noticed

overhear

clothes worn under those that show

undergraduate

to burden someone over or more than what is normal

overthrow

the lower side or the side under the upper surface of something

underwear

to throw beyond or too vigorously, or to remove from power using force

underrate

supervision, or seeing over something without noticing it

overflow

to rate too low or have too low an opinion of something

underside

to hear something without meaning to or without being included in the conversation

Date:

Fluency Focus

Fascinating Bats

Can you imagine a cave full of bats? Tens of thousands of them sometimes live together in one cave! Bats can live in caves, trees, deserts, and even in house attics.

Over the years, bats have had some bad press, especially in horror movies. But bats do not attack humans or get caught in people's hair. Bats are not vicious. In fact, bats are good for the environment. Most cave-dwelling bats eat tons of crop-destroying insects.

Bats are active at night and they rest during the day. How do bats get around in the dark of night? They use their excellent sense of hearing. Most bats can actually see very well, but eyesight is of little use in the dark, so many bats "see" by listening to echoes.

A bat makes high-pitched sounds that bounce off objects around it. The bat listens to the echoes and is able to judge how far away an object is, its size, and if it is moving.

Date:

Character

A **character** is a person in a fiction story. Think about what the main characters **do**, **say**, and **think** to find out what they are like.

Use the information from the story to fill in the character chart.

What Alita Is Like	Story Clues
_____	_____
_____	_____
_____	_____
_____	_____

What Paul Is Like	Story Clues
_____	_____
_____	_____
_____	_____
_____	_____

Use the story and your character chart to write the answers.

1. How are Alita and Paul different from one another?

_____

_____

2. Are you more like Alita or Paul? Explain.

_____

_____

Date:

Vocabulary

Directions: Read the sentences below and decide if each sentence is True or False. Each sentence contains one of the vocabulary words, in bold, that we have studied. Write T or F on the line before the number.

_____ 1. A **cantaloupe** is a melon with a rough skin and sweet, juicy, orange fruit.

_____ 2. When you sing a song, it is important to have the necessary **ingredients** on hand.

_____ 3. When Alita shook a **generous** amount of cinnamon on each quesadilla, she put a very small amount of cinnamon on it.

_____ 4. An **expression** is the look on someone's face. It could be happy, worried, or scared.

_____ 5. If you are confident horseback rider, you are not **doubtful**.

_____ 6. When the cheese **spewed** out of the blender, it flew out with force.

_____ 7. When Alita was **nudging** Paul, she was pulling him towards her.

_____ 8. If you talk to someone **affectionately**, you do not like him at all.

_____ 9. To **complicate** your plans is to make them more difficult.

_____ 10. When Paul and Alita's mother gave Alita an **anxious** smile, she was worried.

Date:

Word Study

Directions: Read the passage. While reading, circle every word containing the prefix 'over-' or the prefix 'under-.' Below the passage, write each word you find in the word column. Define each word in the space next to it, on the right.

On Monday, Marco felt like he woke up on the wrong side of the bed. Not only did he oversleep, but the Florida sky, which was normally a bright blue, was overcast. Marco's Mami yelled that if he didn't hurry up, he would be late and would miss the bus again. Plus, Mami would be late to work and wouldn't be paid overtime. "Marco! Why did you oversleep?" Mami yelled from the kitchen, while Marco still lay in bed in his undershirt and pajama pants. Marco yelled back, "I couldn't tell what time it was, Mami." He blamed it on the dark grey cloud that rested overtop of their house and covered up the sun. Mami opened Marco's door and laughed, saying, "Marco, my boy, I won't underestimate you. You know how to read the clock. Now get out of bed."

Word: **Definition:**

_____   _____

_____   _____

_____   _____

_____   _____

_____   _____

_____   _____

Fluency Focus

Fascinating Bats

Can you imagine a cave full of bats? Tens of thousands of them sometimes live together in one cave! Bats can live in caves, trees, deserts, and even in house attics.

Over the years, bats have had some bad press, especially in horror movies. But bats do not attack humans or get caught in people's hair. Bats are not vicious. In fact, bats are good for the environment. Most cave-dwelling bats eat tons of crop-destroying insects.

Bats are active at night and they rest during the day. How do bats get around in the dark of night? They use their excellent sense of hearing. Most bats can actually see very well, but eyesight is of little use in the dark, so many bats "see" by listening to echoes.

A bat makes high-pitched sounds that bounce off objects around it. The bat listens to the echoes and is able to judge how far away an object is, its size, and if it is moving.

Your Turn to Write

What I Am Like	Clues
_____	_____
_____	_____
_____	_____
_____	_____

What _____ Is Like	Clues
_____	_____
_____	_____
_____	_____
_____	_____

Use the information from your chart to write a paragraph that tells what happened and shows what you and the other person are like.

_____

_____

_____

_____

_____

_____

_____

Date:

Vocabulary

Circle the letter next to the best meaning for each underlined word.

1. In this story, <u>nudging</u> means—
   A smiling at someone
   B laughing loudly
   C talking to someone
   D giving a small push

2. In this story, <u>ingredients</u> means—
   E instructions to make something
   F coupons to save money on food
   G items needed to make something
   H invitations to dinner

3. In this story, <u>anxious</u> means—
   A worried
   B surprised
   C excited
   D unhappy

4. In this story, <u>expression</u> means—
   E something someone does
   F the look on someone's face
   G something someone hears
   H a mistake someone makes

5. In this story, <u>complicate</u> means—
   A to make a recipe
   B to make easier
   C to make difficult
   D to make a joke

6. In this story, <u>cantaloupe</u> means—
   E a kind of recipe
   F a solution to a problem
   G a shopping list
   H a kind of melon

7. In this story, <u>spewed</u> means—
   A poured out slowly
   B flew out with force
   C measured carefully
   D spoke angrily

8. In this story, <u>generous</u> means—
   E friendly
   F selfish
   G large
   H funny

Part A

Directions: Separate each word into its prefix and root word on the lines provided.

Word	Prefix	Root Word
1. illogical	_____	_____
2. imperfect	_____	_____
3. imbalance	_____	_____
4. illegible	_____	_____
5. irreversible	_____	_____
6. irresistible	_____	_____

Part B

Directions: Use three of the words above in original sentences.

1. _____

   _____

2. _____

   _____

3. _____

   _____

Fluency Focus

Mount Everest

If you stood on the summit of Mount Everest, you would be standing on the highest point on Earth. If jumbo jets were to fly over the summit at their normal altitude, a climber at Everest's top could wave to passengers through the windows.

Mount Everest, measured in 1999 using global-positioning satellites, is 29,032 feet above sea level. The Himalayan mountain range, which Mount Everest is a part of, has most of the tallest mountain peaks in the world. The Himalayas are the youngest mountain range on Earth.

Mount Everest was formed about 60 million years ago. As Earth's continents drifted apart, the land mass that is now India collided with the greater land mass that is now Asia. When the two lands met, the impact forced part of the land downward and the rest upward, forming the mountain range of the Himalayas. The Himalayas took millions of years to form. Scientists tell us that even today the mountain range is still shifting.

Date:

Comprehension

Directions: Read the story below and complete the Sequence Chart.

Angie unlocked the door to her neighbors' apartment so she could walk their new puppy, Stripes. The moment she stepped inside, he bounded around the corner, playful as ever. He held a ball in his mouth as if he wanted to play fetch on his walk. Before she even petted him, Angie collected the things she would need for the walk. She grabbed Stripes' leash from the hook near the door. Then, she opened a cabinet and pulled out a plastic bag. Finally, she looked for Stripes' collar to put around his neck.

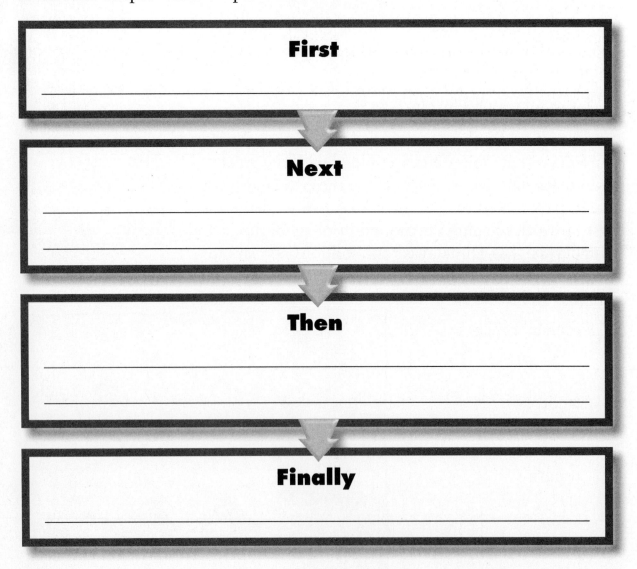

First

_____

Next

_____

Then

_____

Finally

_____

Vocabulary

Directions: 1. Listen as the teacher reads each vocabulary word.
2. Read each word aloud with the teacher.

1. effective

2. era

3. massive

4. muscular

5. obstacle

6. participate

7. remembrance

8. territory

9. tundra

10. vital

Directions: In the Word column, fill in the blank with the correct prefix from the box. Then draw a line matching the word and its correct definition, found somewhere in the right-hand column.

il	im	ir

Word

Definition

1. _____logical

too strong to be resisted

2. _____perfect

lack of balance

3. _____balance

not emotionally developed or mature

4. _____mobile

not movable, not able to move

5. _____legible

not having sense

6. _____reversible

not able to be read

7. _____resistible

rude, not well-mannered

8. _____mature

against the law

9. _____polite

having flaws, faulty

10. _____legal

not able to be turned the other way or altered

Fluency Focus

Mount Everest

If you stood on the summit of Mount Everest, you would be standing on the highest point on Earth. If jumbo jets were to fly over the summit at their normal altitude, a climber at Everest's top could wave to passengers through the windows.

Mount Everest, measured in 1999 using global-positioning satellites, is 29,032 feet above sea level. The Himalayan mountain range, which Mount Everest is a part of, has most of the tallest mountain peaks in the world. The Himalayas are the youngest mountain range on Earth.

Mount Everest was formed about 60 million years ago. As Earth's continents drifted apart, the land mass that is now India collided with the greater land mass that is now Asia. When the two lands met, the impact forced part of the land downward and the rest upward, forming the mountain range of the Himalayas. The Himalayas took millions of years to form. Scientists tell us that even today the mountain range is still shifting.

E8

Sequence

Writers use **sequence** to help readers understand the order in which events happen.

Use the information from the article to complete the sequence chart. Show what drivers must do to participate in the Iditarod race. Write the events in sequence.

First, drivers must qualify for the Iditarod.

⬇

⬇

⬇

Use the article and your sequence chart to write the answers.

1. What happens after a driver gives a command to the lead dog?

_____

2. What happens after the step you wrote in the last box on the chart?

_____

_____

Date:

Vocabulary

Choose a word from the box to complete each sentence.

| obstacle participate remembrance territory tundra vital |

1. The Iditarod Sled Dog Race is held each year as a
   _____ of the original sled dogs that used the Iditarod
   Trail.

2. Today's Iditarod Trail spans across Alaska's vast
   _____.

3. The first _____ for sled dog team drivers is to qualify
   for the Iditarod race.

4. In order to do this, team drivers train hard all summer so they
   can _____ in the race in March.

5. Once the race begins, drivers carry water and other
   _____ supplies.

6. The sled dog teams must be prepared for the long race across
   the empty, frozen _____.

EXTEND YOUR VOCABULARY

Analogies An analogy compares two pairs of words.
The relationship between the second pair must have
the same relationship as the first pair of words.

Write the vocabulary word that completes each
analogy.

| effective |
| era |
| massive |
| muscular |

7. *Giraffe* is to *tall* as *elephant* is to _____.

8. *Runner* is to *fast* as *wrestler* is to _____.

9. *Foolish* is to *wise* as *useless* is to _____.

10. *Day* is to *month* as *year* is to _____.

Date: _____

Word Study

Directions: Read the story. While reading, circle every word containing the prefix il-, the prefix im-, or the prefix ir-. Below the story, write each word you find in the word column. Define each word in the space next to it, on the right.

Angie found Stripes' collar and put it on him, attaching his leash. She pulled him toward the door, but he was immobile and would not budge. Then, Stripes started to pull Angie. She was getting frustrated but laughed at him. "I'm trying to take you for a walk, Stripes, but you're making me imbalanced," she said. She set the leash down and began to pet him.

Stripes ran over to his bowls on the kitchen floor. He dropped the ball in his mouth into one of them. Angie looked at him with curiosity. "I know your Mom and Dad fed you. It's illogical that they didn't," she said.

Stripes picked up the ball again and ran in circles around Angie. Then he ran back over to his bowl and dropped the ball into it again. Angie sighed. "It's impolite to trick someone, Stripes. I'm not falling for it."

Stripes hung his head and sulked. He walked over to Angie and looked up at her with adoring eyes. He wagged his tail and panted. "Okay, Stripes." Angie leaned over to pet him again. "You're too irresistible. I'll get you some more food."

Word: Definition:

_____   _____

_____   _____

_____   _____

_____   _____

_____   _____

Fluency Focus

Mount Everest

If you stood on the summit of Mount Everest, you would be standing on the highest point on Earth. If jumbo jets were to fly over the summit at their normal altitude, a climber at Everest's top could wave to passengers through the windows.

Mount Everest, measured in 1999 using global-positioning satellites, is 29,032 feet above sea level. The Himalayan mountain range, which Mount Everest is a part of, has most of the tallest mountain peaks in the world. The Himalayas are the youngest mountain range on Earth.

Mount Everest was formed about 60 million years ago. As Earth's continents drifted apart, the land mass that is now India collided with the greater land mass that is now Asia. When the two lands met, the impact forced part of the land downward and the rest upward, forming the mountain range of the Himalayas. The Himalayas took millions of years to form. Scientists tell us that even today the mountain range is still shifting.

Date:

195

Your Turn to Write

Think about an activity you like to do. In the chart below, write the steps in sequence to show how to do the activity.

Date:

Vocabulary

Directions: Draw a line from the each word in the left-hand column to its definition, which is located somewhere in the right-hand column.

Words	Definitions
era	necessary to life
muscular	a cold area in which there are no trees and the ground is always frozen
tundra	a period of time in history
vital	having great size or weight
participate	something that prevents one from doing something
territory	an object or activity that makes people remember something
remembrance	working very well
massive	a large area of land
effective	having strong muscles
obstacle	to take part in an activity or event

Date:

Directions: Choose the prefix that will make each word match the definition. Write the prefix in the blank space before the word.

sub	super	over	under	il	im	ir

Word   Definition

1. _____proper   not proper or correct

2. _____flow   to flow over the limit

3. _____total   a total below or part of the larger total

4. _____inflate   to inflate too much

5. _____movable   not able to be moved

6. _____logical   not making sense

7. _____visor   someone who oversees work

8. _____title   a title written below or after the first title

9. _____regular   not normal or regular

10. _____rate   to rate too low or have too low an opinion of something

Fluency Focus

The Thinking Tree

From her thinking branch, Anna could see right over the valley, across the city below. The sprawling tree far from her house had always been her special place—her thinking tree. As a small child, she'd sat on the thinking branch and planned adventures over the mountains to exotic lands. At other times, she had imagined herself talking face-to-face with giants standing far below in the valley, and enlisting their help in times of trouble. Her valley could do with their help now that her country was at war.

These days, when Anna sat on her thinking branch, she mostly thought about the city below. She thought about how it was changing, and she tried to remember how the buildings had looked before the war had started. She often wondered what else might change, so she sketched her favorite places and jotted down memories in her sketchbook. Her thinking tree wasn't such a happy place these days, but it was a peaceful place and, to Anna, it seemed a safe place.

E10

Date:

199

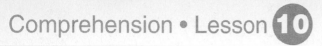

Comprehension

Mark and Nina decided to start a family band. Nina would play the guitar, and Mark would play the drums. They asked their younger sister if she would sing in it. They were not sure whom else they should ask to be in the band. They made a list of other types of instruments that could be in the band. The list included the bass guitar, the flute, the tambourine, the mandolin, and the piano. Their Aunt Nicole played both the flute and the piano.

Prediction:

_____

_____

_____

_____

_____

_____

_____

Vocabulary

Directions: Draw a line connecting each word on the left with its synonym on the right.

Words	Synonyms
abandoned	bag
brittle	plodded
expectantly	amazing
grueling	saying
miraculous	deserted
satchel	single
scouring	fragile
slogan	hopefully
solitary	scrubbing
trudged	exhausting

E10

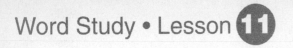

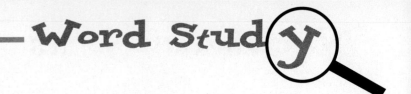

Directions: Draw a line from each word in the column on the left to its correct definition in the column on the right.

Words	Definitions
oversleep	not legal, against the law
illegal	not able to be resisted
subculture	a topic or subject below or within the larger topic
irresistible	rude, not polite
undergraduate	a person below graduate level
overcooked	not mature
impolite	above what is natural
supernatural	to sleep too much or past the time designated
immature	a culture below or within the larger culture
subtopic	cooked too much

Date:

Fluency Focus

The Thinking Tree

From her thinking branch, Anna could see right over the valley, across the city below. The sprawling tree far from her house had always been her special place—her thinking tree. As a small child, she'd sat on the thinking branch and planned adventures over the mountains to exotic lands. At other times, she had imagined herself talking face-to-face with giants standing far below in the valley, and enlisting their help in times of trouble. Her valley could do with their help now that her country was at war.

These days, when Anna sat on her thinking branch, she mostly thought about the city below. She thought about how it was changing, and she tried to remember how the buildings had looked before the war had started. She often wondered what else might change, so she sketched her favorite places and jotted down memories in her sketchbook. Her thinking tree wasn't such a happy place these days, but it was a peaceful place and, to Anna, it seemed a safe place.

E11

Date: © 2004 Education Station, LLC   **203**

Predict

Writers give clues in a story about what action or event will happen next. Story clues can help a reader **predict**.

Complete the prediction chart. Use details from the story that gave clues about what happened in the story.

Prediction
The four friends will help the farm family.

Story Clues That Helped Me Predict

_____

_____

_____

_____

_____

_____

Use the story and your prediction chart to write the answers.

1. What do you think will happen to the farm family after the story ends?

_____

_____

_____

2. What do you think will happen to the four friends after the story ends?

_____

_____

_____

Date:

# Vocabulary

Circle the letter next to the best answer.

1. In this story, <u>trudged</u> means—

   A jumped up
   B walked quickly
   C ran away
   D walked with effort

2. In this story, <u>scouring</u> means—

   E eating
   F cleaning
   G listening
   H planning

3. In this story, <u>brittle</u> means—

   A soft and flexible
   B rough and strong
   C dry and easily broken
   D broken but easily fixed

4. In this story, <u>slogan</u> means—

   E a long speech
   F a book report
   G an advertisement
   H a phrase used by a group

5. In this story, <u>solitary</u> means—

   A alone
   B unhappy
   C a group
   D unusual

6. In this story, <u>miraculous</u> means—

   E depressing
   F strange
   G amazing
   H humorous

E11

Extend Your Vocabulary

Context Clues Sentences often contain clues to the meaning of an unfamiliar word.

Complete each sentence with a word from the box. Write the word on the line.

abandoned
expectantly
grueling
satchel

7. Theo packed his _____ with gardening and cleaning supplies.

8. He was excited and waited _____ for his friend to arrive.

9. The _____ playground had not been used for years.

10. After a _____ day of cleaning and planting, it was ready.

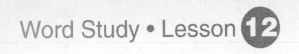

Directions: Read the passage. Then, use the words from the word box to fill in the blanks so that the passage makes sense.

Word Box

illegible	immature	imperfect
irrational	overheard	overtime
substandard	superstar	underage

Emilio wanted to be a(n) _____. He often dreamed of entering a television contest so that everyone in the world would see his musical talent. He had two problems, though. First, he was 12 and the minimum contest entry age was 16, so he was _____. Second, he knew that he was a(n) _____ musician, who did not have enough years of study. He had even _____ his music teacher telling his parents that he would have to practice _____— much more than the two hours he already practiced each day—if he wanted to succeed. Did that mean that his playing was _____? Emilio realized that even the greatest musicians were _____ and made mistakes, but he also wondered if his dreams were _____. He doubted his talent. After all, even the songs he made up were _____ when he wrote them down.

Date:

Fluency Focus

The Thinking Tree

From her thinking branch, Anna could see right over the valley, across the city below. The sprawling tree far from her house had always been her special place—her thinking tree. As a small child, she'd sat on the thinking branch and planned adventures over the mountains to exotic lands. At other times, she had imagined herself talking face-to-face with giants standing far below in the valley, and enlisting their help in times of trouble. Her valley could do with their help now that her country was at war.

These days, when Anna sat on her thinking branch, she mostly thought about the city below. She thought about how it was changing, and she tried to remember how the buildings had looked before the war had started. She often wondered what else might change, so she sketched her favorite places and jotted down memories in her sketchbook. Her thinking tree wasn't such a happy place these days, but it was a peaceful place and, to Anna, it seemed a safe place.

E12

Your Turn to Write

Have you ever wanted to travel back in time? Where would you like to go? What would you do? Use the prediction chart below to plan your story.

Prediction Readers Should Make
____
____
Story Clues To Help Readers Predict
____
____
____
____
____
____

Date:

Directions: Draw a line from each word in the column on the left to its matching definition in the column on the right.

Words	Definitions
grueling	alone, single
trudged	a bag carried over the shoulder
abandoned	with expectation, waiting for something to happen
brittle	walked with effort
expectantly	very demanding and tiring
scouring	deserted, no longer used
solitary	cleaning by rubbing hard
miraculous	wonderful, amazing
slogan	easily snapped or broken
satchel	a phrase used by a group to express its goal or belief

E12

Word Study

Part A

Directions: For each item, add '-ity' to the altered root word to make a new word. Write it on the blank line before its definition.

1. <u>active</u> (activ) + *-ity* = _____: the quality of having energy or action

2. <u>available</u> (availabil) + *-ity* = _____: the state of being accessible or present

3. <u>electric</u> + *-ity* = _____: the quality of having electric current

4. <u>prosper</u> + *-ity* = _____: the state of having success

5. <u>scarce</u> (scarc) + *-ity* = _____: the quality of being rare or insufficient

6. <u>brief</u> (brev) + *-ity* = _____: the quality of being brief or concise; the quality of having energy or action

Part B

Directions: Circle true or false for each of the definitions below.

<u>activity</u>: the state of action	True	False
<u>availability</u>: the state of being invisible	True	False
<u>electricity</u>: the quality of being electric	True	False
<u>prosperity</u>: the state of economic failure	True	False
<u>scarcity</u>: the quality of being rare or insufficient	True	False
<u>brevity</u>: the quality of including every detail	True	False

Date:

Fluency Focus

A Perfect Fit

New technologies often end up in uses that their inventors never imagined. X-ray technology was first invented in 1895. X-rays are special pictures that show the bones inside the body. Soon after they were invented, doctors began using X-rays to help them see into patients' bodies. X-rays are still widely used by doctors and dentists today. However, X-rays have also been used in more unexpected ways.

In the 1950s, about 10,000 shoe-fitting X-ray boxes were used in shoe stores all around the United States. Children would try on shoes and then place their feet in the special box. X-rays were then beamed onto the children's feet. The x-rays produced an image of the feet inside the shoes. Salespeople could show parents just how well the shoes fit.

There was only one problem. X-rays can actually be harmful to human health. In high doses, they can cause burns and cancer. The design of the shoe-fitting X-ray boxes was not safe. The boxes leaked X-rays. By 1970, the shoe-fitting X-ray boxes were banned in 33 states. Today, they are seen only in museums.

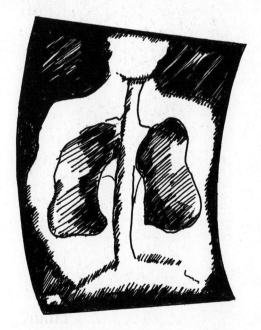

E13

Comprehension

Directions: Read the passage, then compare and contrast Marco and Mami in the diagram below.

On Monday, Marco felt like he woke up on the wrong side of the bed. Not only did he oversleep, but the Florida sky, which was normally a bright blue, was overcast. Marco's Mami yelled that if he did not hurry up, he would be late and would miss the bus again. She knew that Marco hated being late to school, even if it was hard for him to wake up. Mami also hated being late, so she always woke up earlier than she needed to in order to get to work on time. "Marco! Why did you oversleep?" Mami yelled from the kitchen, while Marco still lay in bed.

Marco yelled back, "It's too cloudy to wake up, Mami!"

Mami opened Marco's door and said, "Marco, I won't let you make excuses. Now get out of bed!"

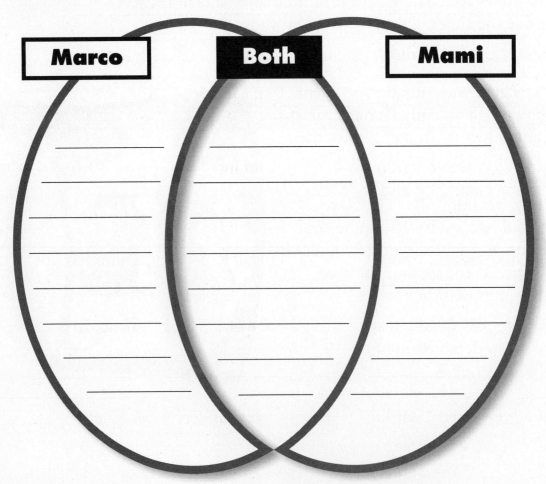

Marco   **Both**   **Mami**

Date:

Vocabulary

Directions: Show what you know. Answer these questions with your vocabulary words.

1. <u>abdomen</u>: Where is your abdomen located? Point to it. _____
    _____

2. <u>afloat</u>: How do you stay afloat in a swimming pool?
    _____
    _____

3. <u>bacteria</u>: What might you do to get rid of bacteria on your hands?
    _____

4. <u>compete</u>: What is a sport in which you like to compete?
    _____

5. <u>digest</u>: What does your body digest? _____

6. <u>hostile</u>: What kind of weather is hostile? _____
    _____

7. <u>lures</u>: Demonstrate how you would lure a fish if you were a worm. You
    may stand up and show us. _____
    _____

8. <u>microscopic</u>: Name an insect you might look at under a microscope.
    _____

9. <u>mobile</u>: What is a synonym for the word 'mobile'? If you cannot think of
    one, demonstrate being mobile. _____
    _____

10. <u>penetrate</u>: What kinds of substances can water penetrate? _____
    _____

E13

Date:

Directions: Based on the definition of each word on the left, separate it into its root word and suffix. Use the definition if you need help spelling the root word correctly.

Word		Root		Suffix	Definition
equality	=	_____	+	_____	the state of being equal or the same
clarity	=	_____	+	_____	the state of being clear
rarity	=	_____	+	_____	the quality of being rare
humidity	=	_____	+	_____	the state of being humid
solidity	=	_____	+	_____	the state of being solid or whole
liquidity	=	_____	+	_____	the state of being liquid

Date:

Fluency Focus

A Perfect Fit

New technologies often end up in uses that their inventors never imagined. X-ray technology was first invented in 1895. X-rays are special pictures that show the bones inside the body. Soon after they were invented, doctors began using X-rays to help them see into patients' bodies. X-rays are still widely used by doctors and dentists today. However, X-rays have also been used in more unexpected ways.

In the 1950s, about 10,000 shoe-fitting X-ray boxes were used in shoe stores all around the United States. Children would try on shoes and then place their feet in the special box. X-rays were then beamed onto the children's feet. The x-rays produced an image of the feet inside the shoes. Salespeople could show parents just how well the shoes fit.

There was only one problem. X-rays can actually be harmful to human health. In high doses, they can cause burns and cancer. The design of the shoe-fitting X-ray boxes was not safe. The boxes leaked X-rays. By 1970, the shoe-fitting X-ray boxes were banned in 33 states. Today, they are seen only in museums.

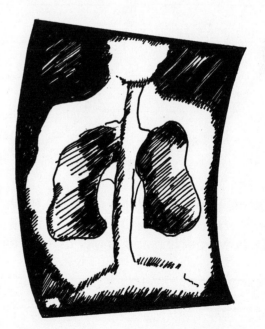

E14

Compare and Contrast

Writers **compare** to show how two or more things are alike. They **contrast** to show how the things are different.

Use the information from the article to fill in the Venn diagram. Under each fish's name, write details that tell only about that fish. Under 'Both,' write details that tell about both fish.

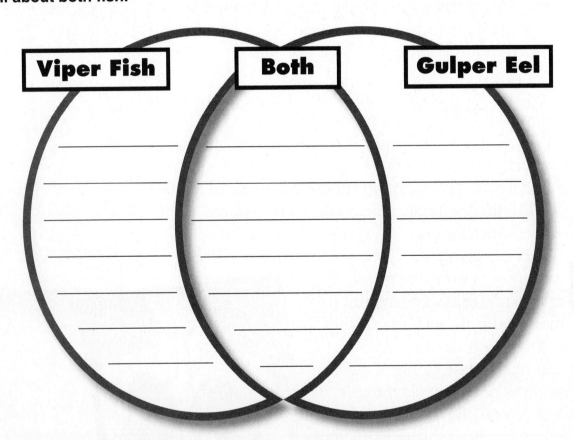

Use the article and your Venn diagram to write the answers.

1. Explain how viper fish and angler fish are alike.

_____

_____

2. Explain how hatchet fish and gulper eels are different.

_____

_____

Date:

Vocabulary

Write the words from the box to complete the paragraph.

abdomen	afloat	bacteria	compete
digest	lures	penetrate	

The angler fish swims slowly along, staying _____ in the deep
1

sea. On its fin hangs a sack of light-making _____. The angler
2

fish spots a small fish ahead and _____ it closer with its light.
3

Quickly, the angler's long, sharp fangs _____ the small fish's
4

_____. Now the angler fish can _____ the food and
5   6

make it last for a long time. It won't have to _____ with the
7

other fish for food until it is hungry again.

Extend Your Vocabulary

Similes Similes describe things by comparing them to other things.
Understanding similes can help you find the meaning of an unfamiliar word.

Complete each simile with a word from the box.

hostile	microscopic	mobile

8. Plankton are as _____ as the cells in your body.

9. The deep sea is as _____ to life as a desert in the summer.

10. Some fish are as _____ as a speedboat racing through the water.

E14

Date: _____   © 2004 Education Station, LLC   **217**

Directions: Read the passage. Use the words from the word box to fill in the blanks so that the passage makes sense. Define each of the words in the spaces below the box.

Alev wants to be a lawyer like her mother and father. Her mother helps people who unfairly lose their jobs because of their religion or race. Her father helps people who are kept from participating in a(n) _____ because they are disabled. Both of her parents fight for _____. They also help others to achieve _____. Every night during dinner, Alev practices speaking with _____. She practices so that when she argues her first court case, people will feel the _____ in the room!

Word Box

prosperity	electricity	equality	activity	clarity

Word   Definition

_____   _____

_____   _____

_____   _____

_____   _____

_____   _____

Date: _____

Fluency Focus

A Perfect Fit

New technologies often end up in uses that their inventors never imagined. X-ray technology was first invented in 1895. X-rays are special pictures that show the bones inside the body. Soon after they were invented, doctors began using X-rays to help them see into patients' bodies. X-rays are still widely used by doctors and dentists today. However, X-rays have also been used in more unexpected ways.

In the 1950s, about 10,000 shoe-fitting X-ray boxes were used in shoe stores all around the United States. Children would try on shoes and then place their feet in the special box. X-rays were then beamed onto the children's feet. The x-rays produced an image of the feet inside the shoes. Salespeople could show parents just how well the shoes fit.

There was only one problem. X-rays can actually be harmful to human health. In high doses, they can cause burns and cancer. The design of the shoe-fitting X-ray boxes was not safe. The boxes leaked X-rays. By 1970, the shoe-fitting X-ray boxes were banned in 33 states. Today, they are seen only in museums.

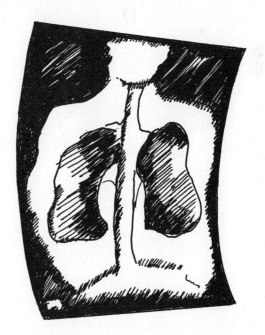

E15

Date:

Choose two animals you know about. Use the Venn diagram below to compare and contrast the animals.

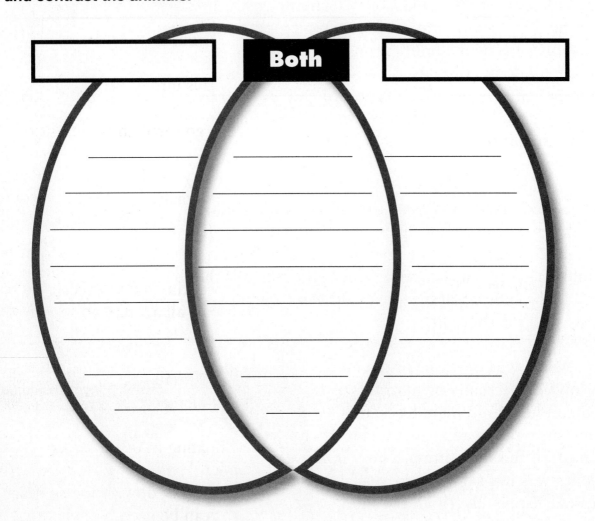

Both

Date:

Vocabulary

Directions: Draw a line from each word located on the left to its correct definition on the right.

Words	Definitions
compete	leads into a trap
lures	to go through something
hostile	to try hard to outdo others at a task
digest	belly
mobile	very tiny living things that exist all around and inside animals
abdomen	too small to be seen without a microscope
penetrate	floating in or on water
bacteria	to break down food so that it can be used by the body
afloat	able to move
microscopic	unfriendly

E15

Directions: For each item, add '-ive' to the root word to make a new word. Change the root word if necessary.

1. mass   +   ive   =   _____

2. react   +   ive   =   _____

3. adapt   +   ive   =   _____

4. effect   +   ive   =   _____

5. destruct   +   ive   =   _____

6. defense   +   ive   =   _____

7. progress   +   ive   =   _____

8. expense   +   ive   =   _____

9. impress   +   ive   =   _____

10. correct   +   ive   =   _____

Fluency Focus

Snowboarding Basics

"Bad luck, Becks. You really packed into the snow that time," a voice called loudly. "Pull yourself up by the toe of your board."

Rebecca spat out a mouthful of snow, adjusted her goggles, and glared angrily at her snowboard, ignoring her cousin John's comment. They had both started snowboarding lessons three days ago, and John was already trying to give her advice. Snowboarding wasn't easy, but Rebecca wasn't about to give up.

Rebecca managed to roll onto her knees and stand up. Now, if she could just learn to stay up!

Looking down the hill, she could see John practicing an ollie. He looked quite stylish, jumping up, catching air, using his arms to balance himself.

Trying to remember what their instructor had told them, Rebecca boarded after John as fast as she dared. She kept her knees bent and her weight over the middle of the board.

"You made it down here without falling. Great job!" John said.

Rebecca felt her confidence building. *I can do this. It's really happening!* she told herself.

E16

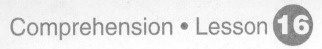

Comprehension

Directions: Read the passage and complete the chart below.

Marlon's favorite activity is making model airplanes. Even though he uses a kit, he can be very creative, so his airplanes are quite impressive. When he invites friends over to fly his airplanes outside, they all have fun pretending to be combative and defensive. He has some airplanes that are massive; they are as big as watermelons! With airplanes that big, Marlon never uses them to be destructive, especially not inside the house!

Inference

_____

_____

Supporting Detail

_____

_____

_____

_____

_____

Date:

Vocabulary

Directions: Read each vocabulary word and think about what it may mean. Make an inference about what the word means, and write your inference in the right-hand column.

Word	Inference
arc	
campsite	
companion	
exasperated	
extraordinary	
horizon	
landscape	
mouthwatering	
secretive	
solar	

E16

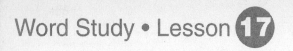

Directions: Choose a word from the word box to complete each sentence.

| disruptive | negative | massive | adaptive |
| active | festive | effective |

1. Holidays, celebrations, and parties are very _____ occasions!

2. In class, it is not good to disturb others or be _____ .

3. If you have a _____ attitude, it will be hard for you to succeed or accomplish things.

4. Stay _____ your entire life for better health.

5. The insects are _____ and survive in almost any environment.

6. That is the most _____ wave I have seen. We had better swim fast!

7. Your speech convinced everyone and was quite _____ .

Date:

Fluency Focus

Snowboarding Basics

"Bad luck, Becks. You really packed into the snow that time," a voice called loudly. "Pull yourself up by the toe of your board."

Rebecca spat out a mouthful of snow, adjusted her goggles, and glared angrily at her snowboard, ignoring her cousin John's comment. They had both started snowboarding lessons three days ago, and John was already trying to give her advice. Snowboarding wasn't easy, but Rebecca wasn't about to give up.

Rebecca managed to roll onto her knees and stand up. Now, if she could just learn to stay up!

Looking down the hill, she could see John practicing an ollie. He looked quite stylish, jumping up, catching air, using his arms to balance himself.

Trying to remember what their instructor had told them, Rebecca boarded after John as fast as she dared. She kept her knees bent and her weight over the middle of the board.

"You made it down here without falling. Great job!" John said.

Rebecca felt her confidence building. *I can do this. It's really happening!* she told herself.

E17

Date: **227**

Make Inferences

Sometimes readers need to **make inferences** about characters and events. Readers can use story clues along with what they already know to make inferences.

Complete the inference chart. Use details from the story to support the inference.

Inference

Ashley has never seen the Northern Lights before.

_____

Supporting Detail

_____

_____

_____

_____

Use the story and your inference chart to write the answers. Give examples from the story to support your inferences.

1. What inference can you make about Ken and his experiences with camping?

_____

_____

2. What inference can you make about Ashley's family and their camping trip?

_____

_____

Vocabulary

Circle the letter next to the best answer.

1. In this story, <u>companion</u> means—

   A friend
   B enemy
   C stranger
   D parent

2. In this story, <u>exasperated</u> means—

   E excited
   F annoyed
   G afraid
   H happy

3. In this story, <u>secretive</u> means—

   A being selfish
   B feeling unhappy
   C making a joke
   D keeping something hidden

4. In this story, <u>solar</u> means—

   E from the earth
   F in the sky
   G from the sun
   H from a fire

5. In this story, <u>horizon</u> means—

   A the line between ground and sky
   B the center of Earth
   C a planet
   D a star

6. In this story, <u>arc</u> means—

   E a large box
   F a curved line
   G a small shape
   H a straight line

Extend Your Vocabulary

Compound Words A compound word is made from two words joined together.

Put two words from the box together to fit each definition. Write each word on the line.

land   site   ordinary   watering   mouth   extra   camp   scape

E17

7. Delicious _____

8. Very unusual _____

9. A large area of land viewed from one place _____

10. A place to set up tents for camping _____

Directions: Read the passage and underline all words containing the suffix '-ive.' Write the words and their definitions in the spaces below the passage.

Marlon's favorite activity is making model airplanes. Even though he uses a kit, he can be very creative, so his airplanes are quite impressive. When he invites friends over to fly his airplanes outside, they all have fun pretending to be combative and defensive. He has some airplanes that are massive; they are as big as watermelons! With airplanes that big, Marlon never uses them to be destructive, especially not inside the house!

Word   **Definition**

_____   _____

_____   _____

_____   _____

_____   _____

_____   _____

_____   _____

Fluency Focus

Snowboarding Basics

"Bad luck, Becks. You really packed into the snow that time," a voice called loudly. "Pull yourself up by the toe of your board."

Rebecca spat out a mouthful of snow, adjusted her goggles, and glared angrily at her snowboard, ignoring her cousin John's comment. They had both started snowboarding lessons three days ago, and John was already trying to give her advice. Snowboarding wasn't easy, but Rebecca wasn't about to give up.

Rebecca managed to roll onto her knees and stand up. Now, if she could just learn to stay up!

Looking down the hill, she could see John practicing an ollie. He looked quite stylish, jumping up, catching air, using his arms to balance himself.

Trying to remember what their instructor had told them, Rebecca boarded after John as fast as she dared. She kept her knees bent and her weight over the middle of the board.

"You made it down here without falling. Great job!" John said.

Rebecca felt her confidence building. *I can do this. It's really happening!* she told herself.

Date: _____

E18

Your Turn to Write

Think of a trip you have made many times, such as walking or riding to school. Use the inference chart to plan a story about it.

Inference I Want Readers to Make

_____

_____

Supporting Details

_____

_____

_____

_____

_____

Date:

Vocabulary

Directions: Draw a line from each word on the left to its correct definition on the right.

Words	Definitions
companion	annoyed
solar	delicious, appealing to the taste
horizon	a large area of land that you can view from one place
campsite	someone that you spend time with, a friend
arc	a curved line
extraordinary	the line where the sky and the ground seem to meet
exasperated	very unusual, remarkable
landscape	keeping something hidden
secretive	a place to set up tents and equipment for camping
mouthwatering	from the sun

E18

Directions: For each item, add '-some' to the root word to make an adjective.

<u>Special rule</u>: When you add the suffix '-some' to a word that ends with a 'y,' change the 'y' to an 'i.'

1. quarrel   +   some   =   _____

2. worry   +   some   =   _____

3. burden   +   some   =   _____

4. flavor   +   some   =   _____

5. lone   +   some   =   _____

6. tire   +   some   =   _____

7. weary   +   some   =   _____

8. irk   +   some   =   _____

9. adventure   +   some   =   _____

10. trouble   +   some   =   _____

Date:

Fluency Focus

Scurvy or Poison?

Scurvy is a disease caused by not having enough vitamin C in the body. Vitamin C is found mostly in fresh fruits and vegetables, and it is important for keeping the blood vessels and red blood cells healthy. In the days of sailing ships, there was no way to store fresh food for a long time. The sailors usually survived on a diet of salted meat, and they often died of scurvy. People who suffer from scurvy feel weak, lose weight, and become bad-tempered. If they are very ill with scurvy, their gums bleed and their teeth become loose.

The symptoms of scurvy are similar to the symptoms of lead poisoning. Lead is a soft metal that was used in pipes for plumbing, and in the finish on pottery in the 19th century. It is very poisonous, but this wasn't known until the 20th century. Severe lead poisoning makes people weak and tired, destroys their appetite, and affects their judgment. The lead ends up in a person's bones and it can stay there for a lifetime.

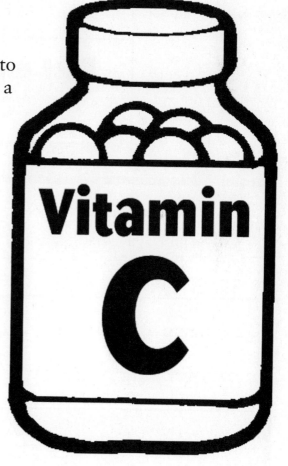

E19

Date:

The twin detectives, Arturo and Alan, were on the hunt for a troublesome kidnapper. They followed him by train to the south of France, where the twosome thought they lost him because of a meddlesome innkeeper who seemed to be helping him get away. The trip had been tiresome, and the detectives needed to rest. It was bothersome to them that they could not catch the kidnapper and save the life of the wholesome woman, whom the handsome Arturo loved.

Fact and Opinion Chart

Facts	Opinions
_____	_____
_____	_____
_____	_____
_____	_____
_____	_____
_____	_____
_____	_____

Date:

Vocabulary

Directions: Read the underlined words, and then answer the questions in the space provided.

1. What kind of flowers could you put in a Hawaiian <u>lei</u>? _____
    _____

2. What is the most <u>magnificent</u> thing you have seen? _____
    _____

3. What type of weather is <u>balmy</u>? _____
    _____

4. What would you use to carve a <u>petroglyph</u> in a rock? _____
    _____

5. Why might you keep your feelings <u>dormant</u>, or hidden? _____
    _____
    _____

6. Name a place that is <u>accessible</u> to people in a wheelchair. _____
    _____

7. What smells like <u>sulfur</u> when it turns rotten? _____

8. What do you call the <u>inhabitants</u> of the place where you live?
    _____

9. Name something you can have different <u>variations</u> or versions of.
    _____

10. What kinds of things have dangerous <u>eruptions</u>? _____

E19

Date:

237

Word Study

Directions: Choose a word from the word box to complete each sentence.

worrisome	wearisome	fearsome	adventuresome
flavorsome		awesome	foursome

1. It was _____ to me that you did not come home on time.

2. The spices in the dish make it quite _____.

3. The monster in the horror movie was ugly and _____.

4. We played tennis as a _____ every weekend.

5. Everyone in the family was _____ after the long plane flight to Hawaii.

6. The clouds outside of the plane looked _____!

7. The hike to the top of the dormant volcano was _____.

Date:

Fluency Focus

Scurvy or Poison?

Scurvy is a disease caused by not having enough vitamin C in the body. Vitamin C is found mostly in fresh fruits and vegetables, and it is important for keeping the blood vessels and red blood cells healthy. In the days of sailing ships, there was no way to store fresh food for a long time. The sailors usually survived on a diet of salted meat, and they often died of scurvy. People who suffer from scurvy feel weak, lose weight, and become bad-tempered. If they are very ill with scurvy, their gums bleed and their teeth become loose.

The symptoms of scurvy are similar to the symptoms of lead poisoning. Lead is a soft metal that was used in pipes for plumbing, and in the finish on pottery in the 19th century. It is very poisonous, but this wasn't known until the 20th century. Severe lead poisoning makes people weak and tired, destroys their appetite, and affects their judgment. The lead ends up in a person's bones and it can stay there for a lifetime.

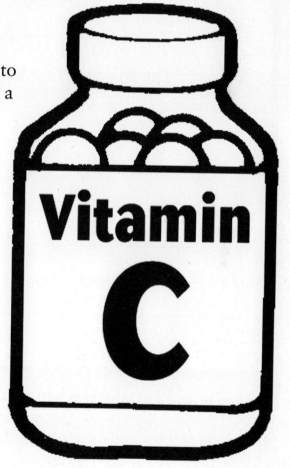

Date:

Fact and Opinion

Facts are pieces of information that can be proven. **Opinions** are personal thoughts or feelings about a subject.

Use information from the article to fill in the fact and opinion chart.

Facts	Opinions
A lei is a native Hawaiian tradition.	Hawaii's islands are magnificent.

Use the article and your fact and opinion chart to write the answers.

1. Choose one fact and explain how you can prove it is true.

_____

_____

2. Choose one opinion and explain how you know it is an opinion.

_____

_____

Date:

Vocabulary

Write the word from the box that best fits with each group of words.

balmy	dormant	inhabitants	lei
magnificent	petroglyphs	sulfur	variations

1. cave paintings, rock carvings, _____

2. necklace, wreath, _____

3. differences, variety, _____

4. gas, fumes, _____

5. impressive, awesome, _____

6. pleasant, warm, _____

7. inactive, at rest, _____

8. natives, locals, _____

Extend Your Vocabulary

Suffixes A suffix is a word part that is added to the end of a word to change its meaning.

-tion = the act or state of	-ible = able to be

Find each word with a suffix. Underline the root word and circle the suffix. Then write the definition on the line.

9.   Some volcanoes are accessible to tourists of all ages.

_____

10. One volcano is off limits due to a recent eruption.

_____

E20

Aa

algae (AL jee) Small plants that grow in water

Cc

camouflage (CAM uh flazh) Coloring or body parts that help an animal look like its surroundings

canopy (KAN uh pee) A covering or top layer

celebration (sel uh BRAY shuhn) A special event or day

colonies (KOL uh neez) Groups that live together

council (KOWN suhl) A group that makes decisions

crest (KREST) Part of an animal's body that rises above its head

cruel (KROO uhl) Mean

Dd

dense (DENS) Very thick

design (di ZYN) To plan how something will look

destruction (di STRUK shuhn) The act of ruining something

detectives (dee TEK tivz) People who find information and solve crimes

Ee

ecosystem (EE koh siss tuhm) A group of plants and animals that need each other to live

endanger (in DAYN juhr) To cause danger

equator (ee KWAY tuhr) The imaginary line around the center of Earth

exhausted (eg ZAWS tud) Very tired

extinct (ex TINKT) No longer living

Ff

fearful (FIHR fuhl) Afraid

features (FEE chuhrz) Parts of an animal's or person's body

fiesta (fee ES tuh) A kind of party

fragile (FRAJ uhl) Easy to break

fringe (FRINJ) A row of thin pieces of fabric or paper that hang down

frisky (FRIS kee) Playful and full of energy

Gg

grasp (GRASP) To take hold of

Hh

harmless (HARM liss) Not able to cause damage

hopeless (HOHP liss) Feeling like the worst will happen

Ii

inactive (in AK tiv) Not active

Jj

jealous (JEL uhs) Wanting what someone else has

Ll

lead (LEED) Helpful information; a clue

Mm

manners (MAN uhrz) Polite ways to act

messenger (MES uhn juhr) Someone sent to give information

misunderstanding (MIS un duhr STAN ding) A failure to understand

mixture (MIKS chuhr) Something made when things are stirred together

Nn

native (NAY tiv) People born in a certain place

nocturnal (nok TUR nuhl) Active at night

Oo

overjoyed (oh vuhr JOYD) Very happy

overlap (OH vuhr LAP) To lay two things together so that they partly cover each other

Pp

predator (PRED uh tuhr) An animal that hunts other animals for food

prey (PRAY) An animal that is hunted by another animal for food

Rr

reef (REEF) A strip of rock, sand, or coral close to the surface of a body of water

relationship (ree LAY shuhn ship) The way animals or things get along together

reputation (REP yoo TAY shuhn) The way people see and think about someone

resolve (ri ZOLV) To settle or solve

ruined (ROO ind) Harmed or damaged

rumor (ROO muhr) A story that has not been proven true

Ss

scales (SCAYLZ) Thin, flat plates that cover the body of some animals

scampered (SKAM puhrd) Ran quickly

scheme (SKEEM) A plan

shed (SHED) To lose or fall off naturally

species (SPEE sheez) Groups of living things that have some of the same features

streamers (STREEM uhrz) Long, thin paper strips

successful (suk SES fuhl) Doing well

sway (SWAY) To move back and forth

Tt

tentacles (TEN tuh kuhlz) Long, thin parts of an animal's body used for moving or feeling

traditional (truh DISH uh nuhl) Something that is passed down from parents to children

tropics (TROP iks) The very hot area near the equator, or center of Earth

Aa

accustomed (uh KUSS tuhmd) In the habit of doing something

affectionately (uh FEK shuhn it lee) In an affectionate or loving way

anticipation (an tiss uh PAY shuhn) The act of looking forward to something

approximately (uh PROK suh mit lee) Nearly; about

attentively (uh TEN tiv lee) Carefully

authority (uh THOR uh tee) A group of people with the power to tell others what to do

Bb

bleachers (BLEECH uhrz) Raised seats or benches arranged in rows for better viewing of an event

Cc

chrysalis (KRIS uh lis) The hard cocoon, or shell, that protects a butterfly during its change from larva to adult

civil rights (SIV uhl RYTZ) The rights of every citizen, no matter their color, race, religion, or gender

cluster (KLUSS tuhr) To stand or grow close together

conservation (kon suhr VAY shuhn) The protection of wildlife and natural resources

conventional (kuhn VEN shuh nuhl) Usual or ordinary

Dd

determined (dee TUR muhnd) Having made a firm decision; showing the ability to stick to a purpose

developer (di VEL uhp uhr) One who builds something or makes something grow

dismantle (diss MAN tul) To take something apart

distinguish (di STING gwish) See or hear clearly; make out plainly

Ee

edible (ED uh buhl) Able to be eaten

emerges (ee MUR jez) Comes out

erosion (ee ROH zhuhn) Being worn away little by little

excess (EK sess) Too much of something

Ff

fads (FADZ) Things people are interested in for a short time

feat (FEET) An achievement that shows great skill

fisheries (FISH uhr eez) Places where fish are raised

Gg

generations (jen uhr AY shuhnz) Groups of people born during the same time periods

Hh

habitat (HAB i tat) The place where a plant or animal naturally lives or grows

Ii

incorporating (in KOR puh rayt ing) Making a part of

inspiration (in spuh RAY shuhn) A sudden bright idea

intently (in TENT lee) In a purposeful or intent way

interpret (in TUR pruht) To decide what something means

majestic (muh JESS tik) Having great power and beauty

migration (my GRAY shuhn) The movement of people or animals from one place to another

molt (MOHLT) To shed feathers, skin, hair, or shell before new growth

nectar (NEK tuhr) A sweet liquid found in many flowers

objected (uhb JEKT ehd) Disliked or disagreed

observed (uhb ZURVD) Noticed something by looking or watching carefully

palate (PAL it) The sense of taste

perish (PER ish) To die

population (pop yuh LAY shuhn) A specific group of animals or people that live in one place

prey (PRAY) An animal that is hunted by another animal for food

prosper (PROSS puhr) To be successful

protests (PROH tests) Displays of disapproval

quest (KWEST) A long search

revolution (rev uh LOO shuhn) A complete change

savory (SAY vuhr ee) Pleasing in taste or smell

scrimmage (SKRIM ij) A game played for practice in sports

significant (sig NIF uh kuhnt) Meaningful or important

simultaneously (sy muhl TAY nee uhs lee) At the same time

solitary (SOL uh ter ee) Living or acting alone

starvation (star VAY shuhn) Suffering from extreme hunger

stationary (STAY shuh ner ee) Standing still; not moving

stylist (STY list) One who arranges or designs something

surpassed (suhr PAST) Better, greater, or stronger than another person or thing

transmit (trans MIT) To send from one person, place, or thing to another

victim (VIK tuhm) A living thing that is hurt or killed

weightless (WAYT lis) Being free from the pull of gravity

Aa

abandoned (uh BAN duhnd) Deserted; no longer used

abdomen (AB duh muhn) Belly

accessible (ak SES uh buhl) Easily approached or entered

affectionately (uh FEK shuh nuht lee) With love

afloat (uh FLOHT) Floating in or on water

anxious (ANGK shuhs) Worried

arc (ARK) A curved line

Bb

bacteria (bak TIR ee uh) Very tiny living things that exist all around and inside animals

balmy (BAL mee) Pleasant and mild

brittle (BRIT uhl) Easily snapped or broken

Cc

campsite (KAMP syt) A place to set up tents and equipment for camping

cantaloupe (KANT uh lohp) A melon with a rough skin and sweet, juicy, orange fruit

chambers (CHAYM buhrz) Large rooms

companion (kuhm PAN yuhn) Someone that you spend time with; a friend

compete (kuhm PEET) Try hard to outdo others at a task

complicate (KOM pli kayt) To make difficult

Dd

descent (dee SENT) Movement from a higher place to a lower one

digest (DY jest) Break down food so that it can be used by the body

dormant (DOR muhnt) Not active

doubtful (DOUT fuhl) Full of doubt; uncertain

Ee

effective (ee FEK tiv) Working very well

enthusiastic (en thoo zee AS tik) Full of interest; excited

era (IR uh) A period of time in history

eruption (uh RUP shuhn) Violent burst

exasperated (eg ZASS puhr ay tid) Annoyed

expectantly (ek SPEK tuhnt lee) With expectation; waiting for something to happen

expression (ek SPRESH uhn) The look on someone's face

extraordinary (ek STROR duh ner ee) Very unusual; remarkable

Ff

fragile (FRAJ uhl) Delicate; easily broken

Gg

generous (JEN uhr uhs) Large; great

grueling (GROO ling) Very demanding and tiring

Hh

horizon (huh RY zuhn) The line where the sky and the ground seem to meet

hostile (HOSS tuhl) Unfriendly

Ii

ingredients (in GREE dee uhnts) The items that are needed to make something

Glossary E

inhabitants (in HAB i tuhntz) People who live in a certain place

landscape (LAND skayp) A large area of land that you can view from one place

lei (LAY) A traditional Hawaiian wreath, worn around the neck

lures (LOORZ) Leads into a trap

magnificent (mag NIF uh suhnt) Very impressive and beautiful

massive (MASS iv) Having great size or weight

microscopic (my kruh SKOP ik) Too small to be seen without a microscope

miraculous (mi RAK yoo luhs) Wonderful; amazing

mobile (MOH buhl) Able to move

mouthwatering (MOUTH wot uhr ing) Delicious; appealing to the taste

muscular (MUSS kyoo luhr) Having strong muscles

nudging (NUJ ing) Giving someone a small push

obstacle (OB stuh kuhl) Something that prevents one from doing something

participate (par TISS uh payt) To take part in an activity or event

penetrate (PEN i trayt) Goes through something

petroglyphs (PE troh glifz) Rock carvings

reliable (ri LY uh buhl) Can be depended on

remembrance (ri MEM bruhns) An object or activity that makes people remember something

satchel (SACH uhl) A bag carried over the shoulder

scouring (SKOUR ing) Cleaning by rubbing hard

secretive (SEE kruh tiv) Keeping something hidden

slogan (SLOH guhn) A phrase used by a group to express its goal or belief

solar (SOH luhr) From the sun

solitary (SOL uh ter ee) Alone; single

spectacular (spek TAK yuh lurh) Remarkable; amazing

spelunking (spee LUNG king) The hobby of exploring caves

spewed (SPYOOD) Flew out with force

stalactites (stuh LAK tyts) Thin pieces of rock that hang down from the roof of a cave

stalagmites (stuh LAG myts) Thin pieces of rock that stick up from the floor of a cave

sulfur (SUL fuhr) A natural element that burns and produces a foul smell

territory (TER uh tor ee) A large area of land

trudged (TRUJD) Walked with effort

tundra (TUN druh) A cold area in which there are no trees and the ground is always frozen

unique (yoo NEEK) One of a kind

variations (VAIR ee AY shuhnz) Differences

vital (VY tuhl) Necessary to life

248